Praise for
The Weekly Coaching Conversation

"Brian Souza is an author after my own heart. Don't miss this outstanding story! Not only is *The Weekly Coaching Conversation* a great story, but Brian also knows that, as a leader, you are nothing without your people. I highly recommend you read this engaging story and let it inspire you to become a better leader."

—KEN BLANCHARD,
Coauthor of *The One Minute Manager* and *Great Leaders Grow*

"Prepare to be entertained, inspired, and educated on what it really takes to begin the transformational journey from acting like a manager to becoming 'a coach.' To get the most out of your organization, team, and especially yourself, *The Weekly Coaching Conversation* is an absolute must-read."

—RICHARD J. BAKOSH, Global Managing Director, Accenture

"Management folklore has a new hero: Coach—a colorful and crusty veteran with tons to teach eager high-achievers. Brian Souza artfully brings Coach to life in *The Weekly Coaching Conversation*, a book grounded solidly in rigorous research and practical experience and written in a highly memorable and inviting style. The fictional world of *The Weekly Coaching Conversation* is packed with real-world dilemmas, timeless lessons, and unforgettable turns-of-phrase. It's a highly enjoyable read, and one you'll find yourself returning to often. *The Weekly Coaching Conversation* is a winner!"

—JIM KOUZES, Coauthor of *The Leadership Challenge*,
Dean's Executive Fellow of Leadership, Leavey School
of Business, Santa Clara University

"*The Weekly Coaching Conversation* is great for the mind and the soul. Powerful coaching!"

—MARSHALL GOLDSMITH,
Author of *MOJO* and *What Got You Here Won't Get You There*

"Every manager, supervisor, team leader, and executive must understand how to facilitate a coaching conversation in order to to get the most out of his or her team. *The Weekly Coaching Conversation* will become the definitive guide on the subject and is destined to become a classic."

—DAVID HUTCHISON,
Senior Vice President, Marketing, SAP Americas

"*The Weekly Coaching Conversation* book and training program has been a game-changer for us in helping to really drive employee performance and organizational productivity. Do yourself—and your team—a favor and read the book and experience the training. You won't be disappointed."

—DAVID SCHNEIDER,
Chief Revenue Officer, ServiceNow

"*The Weekly Coaching Conversation* does a brilliant job of bringing to life how it feels like to be coached the right way. By flipping the perspective found in most business books, it tells an engaging story through the eyes of the one being led. The fable it weaves helps personalize this transformational experience while providing a solid framework, practical advice, and actionable takeaways on how to facilitate a constructive coaching conversation. *The Weekly Coaching Conversation* is an absolute must-read for all managers and aspiring leaders."

—MICHEL KOOPMAN, CEO, getAbstract

"*The Weekly Coaching Conversation* is a great read and will become the definitive guide for aspiring leaders. If you want to take your team's performance to the next level, read this book."

—MARK SILVERMAN, President, The Big Ten Network

"*The Weekly Coaching Conversation* is full of warm, wonderful wisdom with timeless lessons for leadership and personal success."

—BRIAN TRACY, Author, *How the Best Leaders Lead*

"Brian Souza's new book, *The Weekly Coaching Conversation*, is destined to become a classic in the world of business leadership and the pursuit of maximizing human potential. It is an inviting, enchanting, and awe-inspiring parable. I highly recommend Brian's new masterpiece."

—MICHAEL LARDON, M.D., Author of *Finding Your Zone: Ten Core Lessons for Achieving Peak Performance in Life and Sports*

"*The Weekly Coaching Conversation* is a powerful book with an important message for all managers. In addition to a great story, in this book Brian Souza also presents a wonderful framework. I highly recommend it!"

—VERNE HARNISH, CEO, Gazelles, and Founder, Entrepreneurs' Organization (EO)

"I thoroughly enjoyed reading *The Weekly Coaching Conversation* and highly recommend it. Brian Souza is a wonderful storyteller with a powerful message. The ideas presented in this book are the foundation of long-term success and should be required reading for all managers and aspiring leaders."

—JOHN DAUT, Senior Vice-President of Sales, NetJets

"*The Weekly Coaching Conversation* cleverly teaches one of the essential truths of leadership—that it is no longer about you! This book offers frontline managers a way to accelerate their journey while offering experienced leaders a nostalgic reminder of the day they learned this truth and the inspiration to take their game to the next level."

—LIZ WISEMAN,
Author, *Multipliers: How The Best Leaders Make Everyone Smart*

"If you want to learn what it takes to lead and succeed in today's highly competitive corporate environment, read *The Weekly Coaching Conversation*. While it's an engaging story that makes it a quick read, the leadership message is timeless!"

—RICK JACKSON, Chief Marketing Officer, VMWare, Inc.

THE WEEKLY

Coaching

Conversation

A BUSINESS FABLE

about taking your team's performance
—and your career—to the next level

• NEW REVISED EDITION •

BRIAN SOUZA

ISBN: 978-0-9960184-0-1 hardcover
ISBN: 978-0-9960184-2-5 ePDF
ISBN: 978-0-9960184-1-8 ePub

Published by ProductivityDrivers, LLC.
ProductivityDrivers.com

Library of Congress Control Number: 2014908216

Printed in the United States of America

To my amazing wife for all her love, support, and friendship over the years. And to my two beautiful daughters for reminding me what it's all about.

CONTENTS

Introduction

I f you study high-performance teams, it's fascinating to observe the parallels between professional sports and business. There is the intense training, complex strategies, tactical game plans, fierce competition, and, of course, the thrill of victory and the agony of defeat. However, above all else you'll notice one key commonality: They both have world-class "coaches" who are committed to bringing out the best in their teams.

Take a good look at your team. Have you ever felt that your team members had more to give, but you weren't quite sure how to get it out of them? Have you ever thought that they might benefit from a coaching conversation, but you didn't really know what to say or how to say it? Are you looking for that one new idea, that one simple strategy that will take your team's performance—and your career—to the next level? If so, I wrote this book for you.

While the fable you're about to read is fictional, the foundation of the framework behind this book and associated training program is deeply rooted in an exhaustive five-year research project on employee performance that my team and I conducted in conjunction with Ipsos, one of the world's leading research firms.

With our research encompassing thousands of managers and employees from hundreds of companies, we had the unique opportunity to interview, study, and analyze hundreds of world-class leaders of highly productive teams. Ironically, while we were initially in pursuit of a new theory on employee performance and organizational productivity, we accidentally stumbled on something much more profound—a truth so simple in its construct and yet so significant in its application that it has literally changed my life.

In short, in analyzing the critical few key distinctions that separate world-class leaders of high-performance teams from most managers, we discovered that the fundamental difference wasn't necessarily their IQ, strategic vision, or operational prowess, as one might suspect. Surprisingly, the fundamental difference primarily came down to one thing: their approach. They didn't act like a manager; they acted like a coach.

Just as in sports, world-class leaders of high-performance

teams understand that the only way to *systematically* improve performance is through consistently giving constructive coaching and developmental feedback. In fact, dozens of studies—including our own—have proven that there is a direct correlation between the quantity and quality of coaching that an individual receives and his or her level of performance improvement.

In other words, a lot of coaching equals a lot of improvement. A little coaching equals a little improvement. No coaching equals no improvement. This seems pretty obvious, right? Apparently not, because we discovered that 44 percent of employees report *never* having received *any* constructive coaching or developmental feedback. That's right: nearly half of employees aren't receiving *any* constructive coaching or developmental feedback!

Why aren't most employees receiving much, if any, coaching? Even more important, why aren't more managers coaching and developing their teams? As you're about to learn, the answer is surprisingly simple—when it comes to the people side of management, they've never been taught the right approach.

Most managers fail to realize that relying on annual or quarterly performance reviews is not nearly enough to move the needle and that relying on *someone else* to come in once a year and train *their team* won't get the job done. They don't realize that coaching and developing employees isn't an annual event, or even a quarterly event. In fact, it's not an event at all. It's an ongoing process that should be inextricably tied to everything that you—as a manger, supervisor, or team leader—do on a *weekly* basis.

In fact, from a cadence perspective, our research revealed that the optimal level of engagement was to facilitate what amounted to a weekly coaching conversation. Having devoted years to codifying those critical few key behaviors required to systematically improve employee performance, we've distilled them into a simple-to-understand, easy-to-apply, three-step framework.

What exactly does that mean? Where's the system? What's the plan? In short, that's what this book is all about. But this book is also about something else: having a little fun!

Have you ever noticed how most business books have a tendency to lull you to sleep before you get the takeaway? Well, I wanted this book to be entertaining first, educational second. My goal is for you to actually *want* to read this book, not feel that you had to because it was a "gift" from your boss.

Knowing full well that the only thing worse than a boring business book is a bad fable, I decided that if I was going to tell a story, I wanted to tell a good story—no, a great story. I wanted to tell the kind of story that not only motivates the mind but inspires the heart. The kind that makes you laugh, makes you think, and maybe even makes you shed a tear or two in the end. As you'll learn in "the story after the story" in the back of this book, this is a story that is near and dear to my heart.

Regardless of where you are on your leadership journey —whether you're an aspiring team leader, a new manager, mid-level executive, or seasoned leader—I guarantee you'll find yourself in this story and learn some incredibly valuable lessons along the way.

The plot is centered around Brad, a sales manager, who gets an impromptu Ivy League lesson in leadership from an old college football coach at a dive bar. After recently turning around one of the company's worst-performing divisions and being named Sales Leader of the Year, Brad thinks he has all the answers—that is, until he meets Coach.

With the business acumen of Jack Welch and the motivational intensity of Vince Lombardi and Sir Alex Ferguson, Coach is a bundle of contradictions. At one moment, he's jokingly ranting mild obscenities, and the next he's dispensing wisdom like the Dali Lama. At times, he can be as militant as a drill sergeant, and at others as mellow as a Rastafarian. Despite his many contradictions, one thing is certain: *Everybody* loves Coach. As you'll soon discover, Coach shares with Brad a new system that not only transforms his career but ultimately ends up changing his life.

Irrespective of your position, industry, or where you might fall on an org chart, if you truly want to become a world-class leader, you must first realize that the only way you can reach your potential is to first help your team members achieve theirs. Or, as Coach says, you must get it into your head and your heart that *coaching is not merely something that you, as a manager, must do. A coach is someone that you, as a leader, must become.*

BRIAN SOUZA
President & Founder, ProductivityDrivers
ProductivityDrivers.com
San Diego, CA

P.S. For information on how to receive instant access to an exclusive FREE video training series based on this book, please refer to the backmatter immediately following the fable.

THE
FABLE

Party Time

Brad Hutchinson was riding high as he made his way down Interstate 280. His destination was Halftime—a famous dive bar just down the street from Stanford University in the otherwise yuppified city of Palo Alto, California. Brad was raring to celebrate. Just a few hours earlier, he had been named Sales Leader of the Year by the executive vice-president for NPC—a *Fortune* 500 high-tech company—at the company's regional awards meeting. This wasn't just any award. In a results-focused, sales-driven company like NPC, it was *the* award. In a few weeks, the company's CEO would present Brad with the award at the company's annual black-tie gala.

As excited as Brad was, a cloud hung over his achievement. A strange vibe had pulsated through the room when the EVP made his surprise announcement. The applause had been polite but light, and whispered reactions combined to form a murmur that filled the room. For some reason everyone—especially those on Brad's team—had been shocked that *he* of all people had received such a highly coveted award. Everyone, that is, except Brad. As far as he was concerned, his results were proof positive that he had earned it. After all, he had managed to transform one of the company's worst-performing divisions into one of the best in only a year.

For Brad, the award was his crowning career achievement and served as proof that he could transcend his humble roots. His drive and determination to succeed were rooted in his upbringing in a working-class family that at times felt lucky just to have enough milk for the Cheerios, let alone a silver spoon to eat with. After working his way through school and earning his bachelor's degree, Brad landed an entry-level job and quickly rose through the sales ranks. Senior management soon took note of this rising superstar and put him on the management fast-track—which only seemed to increase his appetite for more money, a bigger title, and greater prestige. And the more he raced through life, the more he did it with a singular focus: himself. With that focus, however, came blind spots that would only become apparent in his new management role.

After the regional meeting ended, Brad had invited his team to help him celebrate at Half-time for Friday afternoon Happy Hour. Now as he sped down Interstate 280—swerving in and out of traffic, blaring Black Eyed Peas through his stereo, singing "I Gotta Feeling" at the top of his lungs—he couldn't help but think, *Tonight's gonna be a good night.* He thought for sure that this night would be one of those legendary nights people would talk about and relive for years to come.

In a way, he was right.

Here to Zero

Brad hit the scene at Halftime at 5:15 p.m., bursting through the doors with enough swagger to make Donald Trump seem like an introvert. With neon beer signs plastered on the walls, peanut shells scattered over the concrete floor, and a mishmash of old dart-boards, oversized TVs, and undersized pool tables, Halftime was one of those unique watering holes where an eclectic mix of bar regulars, high-powered business executives, and university students came together to let their hair down and blow off steam.

Brad bellied up to the bar and ordered a pint from Little Nikki. An imposing figure at six-foot-five with a shiny bald head and his signature cutoff T-shirt to show off his bulging biceps, Nikki looked more like the leader of the Hell's Angels biker gang than the affable owner of one of the friendliest hangouts in town.

Brad shucked a few peanuts, throwing the shells on the floor as Nikki slid him a cold draft. He downed it like ice-cold water on a hot summer day. He was there to celebrate, and tonight he planned to go *big*. So he ordered another and managed to polish it off as quickly as the first. With two pints down in less than thirty minutes, he figured he had better hit the head before the others showed up and the *real* party started.

As he made his way to the restroom at the back of the bar, the Black Eyed Peas song still stuck in his head, and he thought to himself, *Yes, indeed . . . tonight's going to be a good night.*

Brad stood over the old tin horse trough, looking over last week's sports section pinned to the corkboard in front of him. Without warning, the door behind him flew open and slammed into the wall.

"That's an awful fancy suit you got on there!" bellowed a gruff voice. "Don't you think you're a little overdressed for a sh-- hole like this? What—you just come from a funeral or something?" The voice broke into a cascade of coarse laughter.

Brad twisted his head as best he could, given the rather peculiar circumstances, and tried to get a look at the man behind the booming voice. He was surprised—and relieved—to see it wasn't one of the rougher-looking guys he'd seen at the bar pounding shots of Jack Daniels at five in the afternoon. This man was older—probably in his early seventies. He was smartly dressed and rather distinguished looking. It wasn't just the way he dressed that said this man was clearly very successful. It was also the way he carried himself—his presence. There was a unique aura about him that instantly put Brad at ease.

"No, not exactly," Brad said as he loosened his tie. "This isn't my usual Friday night getup. I actually just came from my region's annual awards meeting. I'm here to—"

"Awards meeting!" the old man interrupted in a loud but friendly tone. "Did you win anything?"

"Matter of fact, I did," Brad boasted, feeling more relaxed now that he'd finished his personal business. "I had a *huge* year. I absolutely crushed my number. In fact, just a few hours ago my EVP announced that I've been selected as the company's Sales Leader of the Year. And to top it off, this is only my first year as a manager!"

As the old man went over to wash his hands, Brad halfjokingly added, "I guess this management stuff isn't so tough after all."

"I don't know about that," the old man said as they left the restroom and walked toward the bar together, "but that's pretty damn impressive. Congrats! So I take it you're here to celebrate?"

Brad glanced at his watch. "Yeah. In fact, my direct reports should be here any minute now. And don't be surprised if you see me riding that electric bull over there in a few hours. I have a feeling tonight's going to be one of *those* nights."

"Then let me be the first to buy you a celebratory cold one," the old man said as he motioned to Little Nikki for another round.

Brad thanked him for the pint and kept the friendly banter going.

"So what brings an old fart like you to a dive bar like this? You don't exactly look like you're with *those* guys," Brad joked, motioning with his head to a few bikers sitting at the bar.

The old man smiled. "Who? Thrasher? Don't worry. He may look tough, but he's one of the nicest guys you'll ever meet. I'm traveling a lot these days, so on Fridays whenever I'm in town I like to come down here to meet up with a few old friends, throw back a few, tell some lies, and reminisce about the good old days. You know how it is . . ."

No sooner had the old man mentioned his buddies than one of them yelled at him from across the room.

"Hey, Coach!" his buddy called. "You gonna shoot pool or keep trying your tired pickup lines on the new guy?"

The group hanging out by the pool tables roared with laughter and exchanged high-fives. The old man just shook his head and grinned.

"Listen," he said, grabbing his pint, "I'd better get back to my pool game before those jokers start trying to cheat. They know that's the only way they'll stand a chance. I'm like Minnesota Fats—I'm just too damn good!" The old man held up his glass for a toast and added, "Here's to you, kid. Sales Leader of the Year in your first year out of the gate? That's one hell of an accomplishment."

Back on his stool at the bar, Brad glanced at his watch. He thought for sure he had told his team to meet him at 5:30, but here it was 5:45, and no one had shown up yet. *No worries*, he thought, trying to reassure himself. *They'll show. After all, it is Friday at rush hour; they're probably just stuck in traffic or something.* He grabbed his phone and fired off a few text reminders.

Every time the front door swung open, Brad eagerly turned his head, expecting to see one of his team members. But the minutes ticked by and not one of them showed up. *Maybe they got lost*, he thought. So he grabbed his phone again and fired out a few more texts, this time with directions.

Meanwhile, he couldn't help noticing the constant flow of professionally dressed, middle-aged men and women streaming through the doors and making a beeline to the back of the bar where the old man was holding court. Each one greeted the guy with an enthusiastic "Coach!" and accepted his bear hug as if they were long-lost friends.

Who is this guy? Brad wondered.

By 6:15, with no messages and no direct reports to be found, Brad began wondering if anyone was going to show up. *Of course they will,* he thought, desperately trying to assure himself. *Why wouldn't they?* Still, he decided he had waited long enough. It was time to kick things up a notch and really get the party started. He ordered another pint, but this time backed it up with a Purple Hooter.

A few more minutes passed. He checked his phone—still no messages. He glanced at the door—still no direct reports. He ordered another pint, another Purple Hooter, and a plate of nachos. Still no messages. Still no direct reports. Another pint, another Purple Hooter, and a plate of wings. Still no messages. Still no direct reports.

After a few hours at the bar celebrating alone, the harsh reality finally sank in: *They're not going to show.*

Brad's heart sank. *I don't get it,* he thought. *Why didn't they come?* As if to add insult to injury, he couldn't help but look toward the back of the room, where at least a couple of dozen people had now gathered around the old man; the crowd was back-slapping, belly-laughing, and having a grand old time.

Meanwhile, back up at the bar all alone, dazed and confused, Brad was an emotional wreck. His stomach churned and he suddenly felt an aching emptiness inside. *How could one of the best nights of my life turn into one of the worst? Didn't his team understand the significance of this award? Didn't they appreciate all the deals he had closed for them? What was wrong with them?*

Then it hit him: Had *he* done something wrong?

For the first time, Brad felt his once-impenetrable shield of self-confidence crumble. At 8:45 p.m., he closed out his tab and headed to the restroom for a final pit stop before counting his losses and calling it a night.

Growing Pains

The old man deftly banked the nine ball off a side rail and into the far corner pocket. He did a victory dance around the pool table to the hoots of the half-dozen or so friends who were still hanging out with him in the back room of Halftime. The soirée had finally started to die down a bit, but those hanging around were still going strong.

Unbeknownst to Brad, the old man had been keeping an eye on him throughout the evening. Following his celebratory dance, he looked across the room and noticed Brad closing out his tab and then heading toward the restroom. After handing his cue to one of his buddies, he followed Brad into the men's room.

"Hey, kid?" he jokingly hollered as he burst through the doors. "What the hell happened to all those direct reports of yours? You didn't fire them, did ya?"

Brad lifted his face from the sink where he'd been splashing water in his eyes, partly in an attempt to sober up and partly in hopes that it might wake him from this horrible nightmare.

"Oh, no big deal," he said. "You know how it is. I'm sure they had a good excuse. No worries."

The words rang hollow in the old man's ears. In the span of just a few hours, he'd watched as the once seemingly invincible young man had degenerated into a shell of his former self. Feeling compassion for the young manager, the old man decided he had better help.

"Hey," he said softly, "just out of curiosity, would you mind if I ask you a question?"

"Sure," Brad said. "What's that?"

"When we were talking earlier, you said that you crushed *your* number, right? Well, my question is . . . how many people on your team crushed *theirs*?"

With that, the old man abruptly turned and walked away. Brad lifted his head from the sink and stared into the mirror, his face still dripping wet.

"What the hell was *that* all about?" he said out loud. He reached for a paper towel, dried his face, and exited the restroom.

"Hey, wait a minute," he yelled in the old man's direction. "What is that supposed to mean?"

The old man was walking slowly back toward the pool tables, as if to give Brad some time to ponder the depths of the question he had just asked. He turned back to Brad.

"Well, you said that your 'direct reports'—I believe that's how you phrased it—were supposed to come here tonight to help *you* celebrate, because *you* crushed *your* number, right?"

"Yeah, that's right," Brad replied. "What about it?"

"And they didn't show up, did they?"

"No, they didn't."

"So, I was just curious if *they* had a reason to celebrate," the old man said.

The question hung in the air unanswered. Finally the old man continued, asking, "How many 'direct reports' did you say you had?"

"Ten," Brad said.

"And just out of curiosity, how many of *them* made *their* number?"

Brad paused a moment to think it over. "Five," he said. "And most of them probably wouldn't have even made their numbers if it hadn't been for *me* parachuting in at the bottom of the ninth inning to close a few monster deals for them."

"Ahhhhhh . . ." the old man said. "Now I see."

"See what?"

"So that's the reason they didn't show," the old man said under his breath. He looked back at Brad with a smirk on his face and asked, "So how long have you had it?"

"Had what?" Brad asked, surprised by such a random question.

"A.A.M. Syndrome," the old man said without missing a beat.

"A.A.M. Syndrome?"

The old man's mischievous smile helped Brad relax just a little but the next words from the his mouth dealt a clean blow to Brad's ego.

"It's called 'All About Me Syndrome.' It's very common among frontline managers—*especially* sales managers. It's a frightening disease that causes its victims' heads to swell to twice their normal size, making them think they're a hell of a lot smarter than they actually are. It's brutal. I bet it's killed more careers than the Great Depression ever did!"

The old man could hardly contain his laughter. Brad, on the other, was clearly not amused.

"Ha, ha," he said. "Very funny . . . now I get it."

"Do you? Do you *really* get it?" the old man asked, cranking the intensity up a notch. "Tell you what. Since you think you've got all this management stuff figured out, let me ask you another question to see just how much you really get it."

Brad stood silently, waiting. The old man appeared to be carefully choosing his next words. With a piercing intensity, he finally asked, "What is your job?"

The seemingly simplistic question disappointed Brad. Suddenly he wondered why he was even wasting his time with this conversation.

"What do you mean?" he snapped. "Like I told you, I'm a sales manager."

"Okay," the old man said, visibly struggling to maintain his composure. "In your role as a sales manager, what is your job?"

"Isn't that obvious?" Brad quipped. "To make my number."

Having had enough of Brad's pompous attitude, the old man lunged forward like a predator pouncing on prey.

"Wrong!" he shouted. "Your job is not to make *your* number; it's to help your team members make *theirs*."

Noticing that heads were starting to turn, the old man lowered his voice slightly but didn't let up on the intensity.

"You're wondering why your direct reports didn't show up to help *you* celebrate?" he said. "It's because *they* don't have a reason to celebrate. Half of your team failed to achieve their goal. And for the other half who made it, you said yourself that it was basically handed to them. There's no cause for celebrating failure. And there's no joy in celebrating an empty victory that was handed to you."

Brad stood in silence, stunned.

"Kid, you just don't get it, do you?" the old man said. "In your new role, it's not about you anymore; it's about *them*—your team members. It's about *their* dreams, *their* goals, and *their* victories—not *yours*. And until you get that, you'll be just another typical manager who's in it to win it for himself."

"You know what your problem is?" the old man added. "You still think it's your job to be the smartest person in the room. It's not. In your new role, your job is to make everyone else on your team feel as if they're the smartest people in the room."

"What are you talking about?" Brad said in a slightly defensive tone. "I'm not supposed to be smart? I'm not supposed to make my number? Really?"

The old man sighed, unable to conceal his mounting frustration.

"Listen, kid," he said. "Over the years I've seen hundreds of mediocre managers just like you come through those doors in their knockoff suits and cheap Italian shoes, walking with a swagger they have yet to earn—thinking they have all the answers. The truth is, you don't know sh--. You may be a frontline *manager*, but you don't have the slightest clue about what it takes to become a front-line *leader*."

With that, the old man turned and started back toward his buddies by the pool table.

Another Disciple

Brad felt like a UFC MMA fighter barely able to get up from the floor after a series of brutal body blows. But while he may have been down, he wasn't out. He decided to make one last attempt to salvage what little pride he had left.

"Hey, hold on a minute," he said. "I won Sales Leader of the Year, didn't I?"

The old man stopped, turned, and looked Brad dead in the eye.

"I hate to burst your bubble, but to be a leader, people must follow. And the fact that your team didn't show up tonight speaks a hell of a lot louder than any trophy you may put on your mantel."

Brad's heart sank—not just because none of his team showed up, and not just because of what the old man said, but because of *how* the old man said it. He remembered how lighthearted and fun-loving the old man had been earlier in the evening, and it was obvious that Brad had managed to really upset him. Brad knew that the guy was just trying to help. He suddenly started feeling something he hadn't experienced in years—remorse. He also knew something else: The old man was right.

Brad took a deep breath and said, "Hey, listen, I want to apologize if I've offended you. It's obviously been a pretty rough night."

With his emotions running high and plenty of liquid courage running through his veins, Brad decided to let down his guard, stop pretending, and for the first time just open up and acknowledge the truth.

"The truth is . . . the truth is . . ." He took another deep breath and quickly glanced around to make sure no one was within an earshot. "The truth is, you're right. I don't have a friggin' clue about how to be a manager, let alone a leader. You want to know why I parachute in to close big deals for my team? It's because that's all I've been trained to do. I'm a sales guy. When I was promoted, I was basically thrown out there without any real training or coaching and basically left to sink or swim. I'm not sinking, but I'm sure as heck not doing synchronized swimming, either."

"Really?" the old man said, lifting an eyebrow and cracking a smile. "I think you'd look pretty cute in one of those sparkly outfits with your hair all up in a bun."

Both of them had a good laugh, which helped diffuse the tension in the air.

The raw honesty and humility in Brad's response struck a chord with the old man. The old man wondered if the combination of his Irish temper and the Irish whiskey had gotten the better of him. He decided he'd been too hard on Brad, especially given all that he had been through that evening.

The old man had been officially retired for quite some time, and it had been years since he'd taken on a new protégé. The young manager clearly needed help, but the old man took a minute to consider whether he had the time and energy to help, given his other charitable and business interests. Finally, the look of confusion and desperation in Brad's eyes convinced him that he had to get involved. Although he hadn't openly asked for any help, the old man felt compelled to at least offer.

"I like you, kid, so here's the deal," he said. "You seem like you've got some potential, some humility, and a lot of fire. And if you're up for it, I think I can help you out. But only under one condition. . . ."

"Sure, what's that?"

"I want you to promise that you'll pay it forward."

"Pay it forward?"

"I want you to promise me that you'll use what I'm about to teach you to make a positive difference in people's lives—especially your team members. I'll invest in you as long as you promise to invest in them."

Brad took a deep breath. Sure, he barely knew this guy. But he was definitely in need of some serious help, and he had a hunch that the old man could provide it. So he decided to follow his gut instinct.

"Done," Brad said.

With a smile the old man extended his hand. "Mick Donnelly," he said, "but you can call me 'Coach.'"

"Brad Hutchinson," Brad said as he shook Mick's hand, "but you can call me 'Sales Manager.'"

Coach smiled, patted Brad on the back, and said, "Now go home, drink some water, and get some rest. I'll meet you right back here next Friday at 5:30. Don't be late."

As they parted ways, Coach turned and called, "Oh, and one more thing. I want you to do a little homework over the next week."

Homework? Brad thought to himself. But he wasn't about to question his new coach before they even got started.

"Sure," Brad said, "what's that?"

"I want you to chew on this question: Why is it that the best players often make the worst coaches?"

Brad gave him a thumbs-up and headed out the door to hail a cab.

Coach's Secret

fter he had recovered, Brad spent the weekend mentally going over his encounter with Coach and wondering what he'd gotten himself into by agreeing to meet with this mysterious character. But he also felt relief, sensing that this outspoken gentlemen was about to help him conquer some pretty serious management challenges he didn't even know he had. At work that week, Brad—unsure of how to handle the fact that his team hadn't shown up—decided to just play it off as if nothing had happened.

The following Friday he arrived at Halftime fifteen minutes early, vaguely remembering Coach saying something about not being late. He grabbed a stool at the bar next to a sharply dressed woman in her early fifties. The woman casually glanced in Brad's direction—then did a double-take.

"Hey, aren't you that guy Coach was talking to last week?" she asked.

Brad, always good with faces, quickly placed this one.

"I am, indeed," he said. "And I believe you were shooting pool with the guy who made the joke about Coach using his pickup line on me."

The woman grinned and nodded.

"I have to admit, that was pretty funny," Brad added.

"I'm Rita Wang," the woman said, extending her hand.

Brad returned the favor. "I'm Brad Hutchinson," he said with a smile. Brad slid a bowl of peanuts between them and cracked one open. "So, Rita, how do you know Coach?"

"Gosh, we've probably been friends for more than twenty years now," she responded. "I was actually on his team years ago when we worked for a small start-up company together."

Brad recalled that Rita and Coach had interacted more like long-lost friends than former coworkers. "You used to *work* for him?" he said with surprise. "So who were all those other people in the group? Was it someone's birthday or something?"

"Well, we like to say that we're all a part of Coach's crew. At some point in our careers, we've all been fortunate enough—blessed, really—to have been on Coach's team. Whenever he's in town, we all like to spend time with him and thank him for all he's done for us and our careers over the years."

Brad couldn't hide the shock on his face. "But there must have been thirty people back there!"

"And there are probably hundreds—maybe even thousands—more around the world," Rita said. "Coach has touched a lot of lives over the years, both directly and indirectly. He's an amazing human being and by far the best boss I've ever had. I've learned more from Coach about what it takes to lead and succeed in a few Happy Hour sessions sitting right back there in Coach's Corner than I did earning my MBA. And trust me, it was a heck of a lot cheaper too."

Rita took a sip from her glass of wine and asked, "So what about you? How long have you known Coach?"

"Actually, I just met him for the first time last Friday," Brad said. "To make a *very* long story short, I discovered that night that I had some pretty serious management challenges. I guess he thought I could use a little coaching—so he volunteered to help me out. In fact," Brad said as he looked down at his watch, "he should be here any minute now."

"Well, consider yourself a *very* lucky man," Rita said enthusiastically. "If I were you, I'd absorb every word that comes out of his mouth." She paused for a moment, considering Coach's penchant for profanity. "Well, *almost* every word," she added with a chuckle. "If it weren't for him, I'd probably still be stuck in the same frontline manager position I was in when he found me."

"If you don't mind me asking, what do you do now?" Brad asked.

"Me? Oh, I'm in marketing. No big deal."

Rita showed no desire to expand on her resume, so Brad shifted the conversation back to Coach.

"I can't get over the fact that all those people who worked for Coach so long ago still worship the ground he walks on and want to hang out with him," Brad said. "That's unbelievable. Hell, I can't even get my team to share a pint with me, and I'm *still* their damn boss!" Brad cracked open another peanut and tossed it in his mouth before asking, "So what's his secret?"

"That's the funny part," Rita said. "You'd think he was some type of academic scholar or something. He's not. In fact, I don't think he even went to business school."

Rita paused, looking thoughtful as she sipped her wine. "His secret is all in his approach," she continued. "He doesn't act like a manager. He acts like a coach."

"A coach?"

"Yeah, believe it or not, he actually played a couple years of professional football back in the day. But after that didn't pan out, he started coaching college football and eventually became the head coach for a small Ivy League school. After a couple of rough seasons, the long hours and stress began taking its toll on his health and he was forced to quit."

"Wow, that's crazy. So how did he end up in the business world?" Brad asked.

Before Rita could answer, the front door of the bar swung open.

"Coach!" everyone in the bar yelled in unison.

"Well, speak of the devil," said Rita. "I'd better let *him* finish the story."

The secret is all in the approach. Stop acting like a manager and start acting like a coach.

The Moment

Coach made the rounds as he strolled into Half-time, greeting everyone with high-fives and hugs as if it had been months—not just a week—since he'd last seen them. He eventually made his way over to Rita, put his arm around her, and hollered, "Rita! You aren't telling lies about me again, are you?"

"Come on, Coach, you know me better than that," she said. "Of course I am!"

Coach laughed. "Yeah, just remember you still owe me five bucks from that whippin' I gave you shootin' pool the other night, and I don't want to hear any excuses, either. Now that you're a big-time CMO, you shouldn't have any problem coming up with the cash."

Then Coach looked at Brad.

"Sales Manager! How the hell are ya?" Coach nearly shouted. "Looks like you finally recovered from all those Purple Tweeters you were drinking the other night. That's sure some pretty hard stuff, isn't it? It'll knock you on your a-- if you're not careful!"

Brad laughed, along with everyone else in the bar.

"No kidding," Brad said. "I noticed Thrasher drinking all the JD, so I figured a Purple Hooter was the next best thing."

Thrasher cast a quizzical look in Brad's direction. He could barely remember where he was last Friday, let alone who this young yuppie punk was that somehow knew his name.

With the universal "I need two pints" hand signal, Coach motioned to the far side of the bar where Little Nikki was clearing away some empty glasses. "Comin' your way, Coach," he said.

When their pints arrived, Brad and Coach made their way back to the far corner of the bar, where Brad noticed a four-inch bronze plate on the wall above a booth that read, "Coach's Corner." On the opposite wall was a giant chalkboard. The side walls were pinned with dozens of celebratory pictures of Coach and his crew that had been taken at Halftime over the years.

"Take a seat, Sales Manager," Coach said as he slid into the booth. "So . . . pretty interesting week last week, huh?"

"Yeah, it was pretty rough on a lot of levels," Brad replied sheepishly.

"Did you have a chance to noodle on some of the things we talked about?"

"I did, and let's just say I didn't get a whole lot of sleep," Brad said. "I just kept thinking about what you said—that I was acting like every other mediocre manager who's in it to win it for himself."

"And?" Coach prompted.

"It's true. That's how I've been acting, but that's not who I am," Brad said. "I don't want to be just another crappy manager. I want to be a leader. And I don't want to have to wait another ten or fifteen years to figure it out. I want to make it happen now."

Coach tossed a peanut about four feet into the air and caught it effortlessly in his mouth when it came down.

"Look, kid, I hate to break it to you, but you ain't gonna become Winston Churchill overnight. Becoming a world-class leader is a process that takes time. And given that we only have a few weeks together, we have two goals: First, I want to teach you the single most important thing that you need to know about taking your team's performance—and your career—to the next level. And second, I want to make sure you're completely prepared so that when your leadership moment finally arrives, you're ready for it."

"Leadership moment?"

"Make a note," Coach said. "One of the keys to succeeding in life is to be ready when your time comes. Everything you do, everything you learn, and everything you experience is all preparing you for that one critical moment. I call it the *leadership moment*. Think of it as a rite of passage that all great leaders must go through. George Washington had his at Valley Forge; Gandhi had his on the Salt March; Rosa Parks had hers on a bus; and Mother Teresa had hers on the streets of Calcutta. It's that split second in time when one's preparedness is challenged, one's character is tested, and one's destiny is determined. It's the very first time people follow you—not because they *have to*, but because they *want to*."

Brad reached into his pocket for a pen, but he had nothing to write on.

Coach, who'd apparently anticipated this moment, pulled out a new pocket-sized journal and handed it to Brad.

"I don't have many rules, but here's one that's non-negotiable: Never come to one of my coaching conversations without this journal," he said. "In fact, don't go anywhere without it. I have mine with me twenty-four-seven." He pulled a tattered-looking journal from his pocket and held it up.

Brad took his new journal and jotted down some notes as Coach moved on to another random question.

"What do you think of the frogs?"

"The frogs?"

"Yeah, you know, the French."

Brad stammered, unsure of where the old man was going with this. "Well, I . . ."

"Yeah, that's what I thought. Anyway, there's one Frenchman I respect and that's Napoleon—not because of his morals or values, but because of his leadership qualities and how successful he was at such a young age. Did you know that Napoleon became a general at twenty-four, ruler of France at thirty-three and emperor at only thirty-five? Do you want to know how he did it?"

"Let me see, if memory serves me, he did it by having short-man's disease and picking fights with his neighbors."

Coach chuckled, but kept on point.

"There was one transformational event—a leadership moment early in his career during the Battle of Toulon that changed everything for Napoleon. That singular event not only changed how everyone else saw Napoleon, but more importantly, it changed how Napoleon saw *himself*. For the first time, he didn't just *think* he had what it took to become a leader—he *knew* it."

Coach leaned forward in his seat, his eyes wide. "Napoleon's troops were outnumbered ten to one, and defeat appeared imminent. Napoleon realized he couldn't wait on orders from Paris, so he decided to step up and take charge. With rain pouring down, he mounted his horse, rode out in front of his troops, and shouted. 'Gentlemen, it looks like history has made room for us after all! If any of you don't feel like going, that is fine . . . I do! I'll take this fort alone and destiny will be waiting. . . . Bullets will bounce off me. . . . Cannonballs will swerve with fear. . . . Not one of you need take this fort, but I absolutely *insist* you come with me and watch *me* take it. . . . If I go forward, follow me. . . . If I retreat, shoot me. . . . If I am killed, avenge me!'

"With that, Napoleon led the charge. Toulon fell, saving the French Revolution and forever memorializing Napoleon's place in history."

Coach's horrible attempt at a French accent echoed throughout the bar as Brad and everyone else in the bar started to laugh.

"Ohhhhh . . . now I get it," Brad said. "You want me to start riding around the office on horseback, wearing a silly little hat, sipping on Beaujolais, yelling *Charge!*"

"Okay, smart a--, are you done?" Coach asked.

"Sorry, Coach," Brad said with a chuckle. "Couldn't resist."

"Seriously," Coach said. "I want you to absorb what

I'm teaching you so that when your leadership moment arrives, you're prepared to seize it."

"How will I know when my leadership moment arrives?" Brad asked. "What if I miss it?"

"Trust me—you'll know. The only question is, will you be ready? Will you step up and seize the moment to prove to yourself and everyone else that you have what it takes to become a world-class leader? Or will you be like most mediocre managers who fail to live up to their potential? Only time will tell, kid. But when that moment comes and it's just you standing on that stage—all alone in the spotlight—you are the only one who will have the power to make it happen."

Empty the Cup

Brad headed to the restroom and was on his way back when Rita nearly bumped into him.

"Hey, Brad," Rita said. "How's it going back there?"

"Great; I'm learning tons about the French Revolution," Brad said with a smile.

Rita laughed, having heard Coach's Napoleon story more times than she'd care to remember.

"Hey, I almost forgot to mention," she said, "be sure to ask Coach about the time he almost got fired from his first management job."

As Rita walked away from Brad toward the other side of the bar, she added in a loud voice, "Oh, and don't forget to ask him about his secret system!"

Brad walked back to the Coach's Corner, but before he could even sit down, Coach said, "I saw you chatting with Rita. What was that all about?"

"I don't know, something about you almost getting canned from your first management job."

"Next to salespeople, marketing people have the biggest damn mouths, I tell you. I bet she also told you about my story, didn't she?"

Not wanting to throw his new friend under the bus, Brad responded, "She didn't go into too much detail. But I'd love to hear it."

"All right," Coach said, glancing at his watch. "I guess we've got enough time for me to give you the *Reader's Digest* condensed version."

Coach explained that he'd grown up idolizing his father, who was a successful high school football coach, and how he'd always wanted to follow in his footsteps. After a successful playing career and a few years as an assistant, Coach landed his dream job: head coach at his Ivy League alma mater. But the university wasn't as committed to winning as he was, and as the losses started to pile up, his stress continued to mount. Eventually, his doctor recommended he find a different career before he suffered a serious heart attack.

"After I hung up my whistle and left the sidelines for good, I was devastated," Coach said. "I was already in my late thirties, and all I'd ever known was coaching. I had absolutely no idea what the hell I was going to do next.

Lucky for me, an old college football teammate happened to be an executive for a communications firm in New York. Somehow he managed to help me land a job as an operations manager with his company."

"Really?" Brad said. "Did you have any management experience?"

"Nope."

"Wow, that's crazy. So how did you pull it off?"

"I didn't, at first. In fact, my new career in management was almost over before it even began. After about six months it became apparent to everyone—especially my team—that I had absolutely no idea what the hell I was doing."

"So what did you do?"

"I panicked. That's when I started devouring every management and leadership book I could find. You name it, I read it. But nothing seemed to speak to me; nothing worked. Finally, one day I'd had enough. I walked up to my buddy's office and told him I was going to quit."

"Are you serious?" Brad said. "What did he say?"

"He looked me in the eyes and said something that completely changed my life. He said, 'Listen, Mick. I didn't stick my neck on the line for you because I thought you'd make a good *manager*. I stuck my neck on the line for you because I knew you'd make a great *coach*. So do us both a favor. Stop trying to be something you're not. Stop trying to act like a *manager* and start acting like a *coach*.' And boom! Just like that, it hit me. I made a decision then and there that I had to change my approach."

"What an amazing story," Brad said. "So is this where the secret system that Rita was telling me about comes in?"

"Easy, big shooter," Coach said. "One step at a time. Let's not get ahead of ourselves. I believe you had some homework to do. Did you do it?"

"Yep."

"Okay, so what are your thoughts?"

"Well, I guess I'm a little confused," Brad said. "The other night I came in here feeling pretty good about myself—like I had all this management stuff all figured out. But after my team stood me up and you burst my bubble, I guess I left with a lot more questions than answers."

Coach nodded in approval. "Make a note," he said. "As a leader, your job is not to have all the right answers; it's to ask all the right questions. Speaking of which, have you ever heard about the scholar who traveled to Tibet to discuss Buddhism with a wise old monk?"

By now Brad was getting used to Coach's rather unique style of coaching, so he simply said "No" without even looking up from his notebook.

"As soon as the scholar arrived at the monastery," Coach continued, "the monk invited him inside to have a cup of tea. While the monk prepared the tea, the scholar began spewing all that he had learned about Buddhism while studying at the university. On and on he kept rambling, trying to impress the monk with how much he knew about Buddhism. Meanwhile, the wise old monk just quietly listened as he prepared the tea. When the tea was finally ready, the monk began to pour it into the scholar's cup as the scholar continued lecturing. He continued pouring the tea, even though the scholar's cup was already overflowing. When the hot tea ran off the table and onto the scholar's leg, he jumped out of the chair and shouted, 'You old fool! What the hell are you thinking?' The old monk calmly replied, 'A cup that is already full has no room to receive.'"

Coach reached for a handful of peanuts.

"I'm not following you," said Brad with a puzzled look. "I thought my homework was to think about why the best players often make the worst coaches. Is there some sort of connection here?"

"There is," said Coach. "The best players often fail to make the leap from player to coach because they fail to empty the cup. Think about it. Michael Jordan, the greatest basketball player who ever stepped on a court, failed miserably as head of basketball operations for the Washington Wizards. Wayne 'The Great One' Gretzky spent four years as head coach of the NHL's Phoenix Coyotes and failed to make the playoffs even once. Diego Maradona, one of the best soccer players to ever step onto the pitch, was fired after just eighteen months as head coach of Argentina's national team—and he even had Messi!"

"I think I see what you're saying," Brad said. "When they transitioned from their role as an individual contributor into the new role of a coach, they thought they had it all figured out. Their cup was full, so to speak."

"Exactly," Coach said. "Along those lines, here's another little nugget you may want to jot down: To succeed at the next level, you must realize that the rules of the game have changed—and so, too, must you. If you really want to take your team's performance—and your career—to the next level, you're going to need a new playbook, a new system."

"All right, already!" Brad blurted out. "What's this secret system I keep hearing about?"

Coach took a quick look around. In a voice slightly above a whisper, he raised his eyebrows and said, "You really want to know, huh?"

Brad nodded with eager anticipation.

*The first step to becoming
a world-class leader is to realize that
the rules of the game have changed—
and so, too, must you.*

"Okay, so you know how they say patience is a virtue, right?"

Brad hung on every word uttered out of the old man's mouth, anticipating something truly profound.

"Well, why don't you be a virtuous young lad and get this old fart another pint while I sit here waiting patiently."

Coach roared with laughter, and Brad just shook his head as he grudgingly made his way back up to the bar.

A New Approach

While Brad was at the bar waiting for another round of drinks, Coach was busy jotting down questions on the back of an old flyer that had been pinned to the wall. Then he grabbed a cocktail napkin and sketched out a simple chart composed of four squares. When Brad returned with their drinks, Coach pulled a sheet of paper from his tattered journal.

"Here," Coach said, handing the paper to Brad. The noise level in the bar had grown louder as the Friday Happy Hour got rolling, so Coach raised his voice against the commotion. "I want you to answer these questions."

Brad scanned the sheet, noticing ten questions along the lines of *On a scale from 1 to 5, how confident are you that your team trusts you and believes that you genuinely have their best interests in mind?*

Brad looked up from the paper. "These are some interesting questions, but I don't see how this has anything to do with me doing my job and making my number," he said somewhat defensively.

"Trust me," Coach said. "This has *everything* to do with you doing your job and making your number."

Brad quickly plowed through the list, answering the questions. He handed the sheet back to Coach.

Staring intently through the reading glasses on the tip of his nose, pen in hand, Coach looked more like a university professor grading a student's pop quiz. Using the sketch he'd drawn on the napkin, he tallied Brad's responses by making a mark next to one of the four squares, depending on how Brad answered each question. Brad watched and wondered until finally Coach took off his reading glasses and looked up.

"Yep, I knew it," Coach said, exhaling loudly. "You're a classic Do-It-All Manager."

Brad was both curious and defensive.

"Do-It-All Manager?" he said.

Coach calmly slid the napkin his way.

"I've been coaching managers into leaders since long before you were even a twinkle in your mother's eye," he said. "And if there's one thing I've learned, it's that there are basically four types of managers. Just by asking a handful of questions, I can pinpoint a manager's approach in only a few minutes. Want to know what's even more interesting?"

"What's that?"

"If you ask the manager's team the same set of questions, nine times out of ten there's a huge disconnect between how managers think they're doing and how well their *team members* think they're doing. Here's the sad part: Most managers are completely oblivious to the impact their approach is having on their team members and their team members' level of performance."

MANAGEMENT APPROACH
MATRIX

	PRODUCTIVITY	
DO-IT-ALL MANAGER		THE COACH
MICRO-MANAGER		NICE-GUY MANAGER

RAPPORT

Coach tapped his finger on the four-square matrix, his eyes fixed on Brad.

"Each type of manager has a very distinctive style or approach that impacts his or her rapport with the team and the team's level of productivity—or performance. Let me give you a few quick examples. When you think of the term *micromanager*, what immediately comes to mind?"

"I think of that annoying boss in the movie *Office Space*," Brad said without even thinking about it. "You know, the guy with the huge glasses and the obnoxious suspenders that keeps bugging Peter about putting a cover sheet on his TPS report."

The look on Coach's face indicated he'd obviously never seen the movie.

"Okay, well, anyway," Brad went on, "I think of someone who's anal . . . who's always right . . . you know, always in your business."

"That's right," Coach said. "Micromanagers are quick to correct and slow to praise. The fatal flaw of the micromanager is that subconsciously they don't trust in their team members' ability to get the job done without them. As a result, they micromanage the work until it's done perfectly—just the way *they* would do it. As a result, micromanagers are perceived as being distrustful, controlling, uncaring, and bossy, right? So let me ask you: How do you think this particular management approach makes the people on the team *feel*?"

"I guess it makes them feel stressed out . . . frustrated . . . resentful . . . unmotivated . . . and unhappy."

"And how does having to work in an environment that makes a team member feel stressed out, frustrated, resentful, unmotivated, and unhappy impact the team's level of performance?

"Not in a good way," Brad said.

"Exactly," Coach said. "The micromanager's overly engaged approach causes his or her team members to put forth just enough effort to skate by—to fly below the radar in hopes of collecting another paycheck. For those team members, it's not a career—it's just a job."

Coach then pointed to the box in the bottom left corner labeled *Micromanager*.

"With that kind of approach," Coach said, "is it any surprise that micromanagers have the lowest level of rapport with their team members and get the least out of their team?"

"Nope," Brad agreed.

Coach next turned his attention to the box in the lower right corner.

"So what comes to mind when you think of a *Nice-Guy Manager*?" he asked.

"I think of someone who's laid-back, mellow, hands-off—maybe even at times a little disengaged," he said.

"Good. Nice-Guy Managers are friendly, non-confrontational, and easy to work for. Their fatal flaw is that subconsciously they're more concerned with being liked by their team members than they are in getting results from them," Coach said. "And when a manager's approach is *too* laid-back or *too* hands-off, how do you think that impacts the team's performance?"

"I don't know; I guess if that kind of manager isn't challenging and pushing the team enough, they obviously won't be learning, growing, or improving," Brad said. "And because those kinds of managers shy away from confrontation, they probably also have a challenge holding their team members accountable."

"You're learning, Sales Manager," Coach said. "Good work."

Coach then turned his attention to the box in the upper left corner. With a smirk on his face, Coach said, "Now here's one that shouldn't be too hard for you to figure out: The *Do-It-All Manager*. How would you describe your—er, excuse me—this management approach?"

"Very funny," Brad said.

Coach waited for an answer, but Brad just sat there silently with his arms folded across his chest.

"Look," Coach said, "I'm not here to tell you what you *want* to hear; I'm here to tell you what you *need* to hear. Everything I'm teaching you is preparing you so that when your leadership moment comes, you can step up and make it happen—because you never know when, or if, you'll get another chance. So you can either listen and learn or not. The choice is yours." After a short pause, Coach asked, "Shall I continue?"

Brad took a deep breath, uncrossed his arms, and nodded a bit sheepishly.

"Okay, then," Coach continued. "The fatal flaw of the Do-It-All Managers is that they *over*estimate their own abilities while *under*estimating the capabilities of their team members. As a result, they have a tough time delegating. They subconsciously believe *if you want it done right, you'd better do it yourself.* They drive results and get things done by taking over. As far as their level of engagement is concerned, they're either all over it or completely absent. Do-It-All Managers are often perceived as being arrogant, selfish, egotistical, distant, uncaring, cold, cocky—"

"All right, all right," Brad said, cutting Coach off. "Enough already. I get your point."

Coach, however, wanted to make sure he really drove the message home.

"This is important," he continued. "I want you to imagine that *this* is your reality. Forget about your perspective for a minute and put yourself in your team members' shoes. How do you think your current management approach makes them feel?"

Brad resisted the urge to roll his eyes. "I don't know," he said. "I guess it might make them feel frustrated and unmotivated."

Coach sat across the table and said nothing, purposely creating a long, awkward silence.

"And," Brad added after giving it some more thought, "I guess they might feel a little unappreciated . . . undervalued . . . unimportant . . . and maybe even a little sad."

Coach softened his tone. "And if your team members come to work feeling frustrated, unmotivated, unappreciated, undervalued, unimportant, and maybe even a little sad, how might that impact your relationship with them? How might it affect their level of performance? How might that weigh on their self-confidence, their pride, and their sense of worth? How might that spill over into their personal lives and affect their family?"

Brad felt his eyes tearing up and quickly looked away.

When he looked back at Coach, he pushed past the lump in his throat and finally tried to answer the question.

"You know, I've never thought of it that way," he said, gazing into the distance as if he were talking to himself. "I've really never thought of it that way. . . ."

"You see, at the end of the day it's not all about the numbers," Coach said. "In the short run, you may manage to put some points on the board and place some trophies on the mantel, but that's just because you're hogging the ball and stealing all the glory."

Coach continued, "I want you to always remember something. When all is said and done and we've completed this journey we call life, what will matter most is not what we have achieved, but rather who we have become."

Please note: if you are interested in learning the critical few key distinctions that separate world-class leaders of high-performance teams (or "coaches") from most managers— download our FREE special report at

ProductivityDrivers.com/FREEReport

When all is said and done and we've completed this journey we call life, what will matter most is not what we have achieved, but rather who we have become.

The Next Level

Veronica Sanchez, one of the old man's friends, approached Coach's Corner, eyed the two men sitting at the table, and immediately sensed some tension.

"I hate to interrupt such a festive conversation," she blurted out, "but I'd like to remind that this *is* a bar and that *some* people come here to have a good time."

Brad, still reeling from coming face-to-face with the reality of how his current management approach was hurting his team, did his best to muster a smile.

Veronica put her hand on Brad's shoulder.

"Don't feel bad," she said reassuringly. "All of us have been on the receiving end of this coaching conversation many times over the years. Coach may make Jack Welch look like a pussycat at times, but I guarantee if you do what he says, it'll not only improve your team's performance, it just may change *your* life."

"What the hell is this, an infomercial or somethin'?" Coach jokingly barked, cutting Veronica off before her flattery made him even more uncomfortable. "Get back over there and start warming up those darts. I'll be over in a sec to give you a chance to redeem yourself."

As Veronica walked away, Coach returned his attention to his new protégé.

"Now where was I?" he continued.

"I don't know," Brad said, "but I'm hoping you're going to tell me how to change my management approach, because right now I'm feeling like a pretty big jerk."

"Oh, yeah, now I remember," Coach said, pointing to the upper right-hand quadrant on the napkin. Here we have the *Coach*."

"As you can see here," he continued, "unlike the others, the Coach is able to consistently get his or her team to perform at the highest level, while at the same time maintaining the highest level of rapport. I can assure you that this is no coincidence. The two go hand in hand."

"How so?" Brad asked.

"Make a note," Coach said. "Great Coaches consistently get the most *out* of their people because they consistently put the most *into* their people. They believe in their people, want them to succeed, and are committed to helping their team members achieve their potential."

Great coaches consistently get the most out of their people because they consistently put the most into their people.

Brad scribbled notes as fast as he could.

"Let me ask you a question," Coach said. "Hypothetically speaking, what if you stopped acting like a manager and started acting like a coach? How do you think this new approach might affect the dynamics of your relationship with your team members?"

Brad took a deep breath while he pondered the possibilities. "Well, for starters they'd probably feel more valued . . . trusted . . . appreciated . . . empowered . . . and maybe even a little fired up to come to work."

"And what if you could create the type of environment where your people felt valued, trusted, appreciated, empowered, and fired up to come to work?" Coach asked. "How might that impact their performance? Better yet, how might that impact *your* performance?"

Brad got the point, but he hesitated before responding. "I don't know; I guess I'm still having a tough time envisioning myself as a leader," he confessed. "I mean, when I think of leadership, I don't think of a lowly frontline manager like me way down in the trenches. I think of the bigwigs up in the ivory tower who are making all the strategic decisions."

"Listen, when you've been around as long as I have, you'll realize that strategy ain't sh-- without execution. Let the big cheeses worry about crafting the organizational vision, strategy, and plan. As a frontline leader, it's your job to get bottom-up buy-in on that plan, execute the strategy, and transform that vision in into reality. *You* are the critical piece in the puzzle."

"Easier said than done," Brad replied. "I must have told my team what to do a thousand times. They know what to do—they're just not doing it."

"Make a note," Coach said. "Leaders don't just tell their people what to do. They invest the time to understand their people and to align their team members' personal goals with the company's goals. Frontline leaders help bridge the gap between what the company wants and what their team members want, making sure that everyone is onboard and rowing in the same direction."

Coach paused, thought for a moment, and then leaned forward for added emphasis.

"Before I forget, I want to make an important distinction that few very people understand," he said. "Coaching is not merely something that you, as a manager, must do. A coach is someone that you, as a leader, must become."

"Wow, that's pretty profound stuff," Brad said. "The way you're describing this new management approach, it seems like a no-brainer. But if that's the case, then why aren't there more coaches? I mean, why are there so many bad managers out there?"

*Coaching is not merely something
that you, as a manager, must do.
A coach is someone that you,
as a leader, must become.*

"There may be a lot of bad managers, but most of them are not bad people," Coach said. "In fact, most of the time it's not even their fault. When it comes to the people side of management, they've simply never been taught the right approach. Most managers have never been taught one of the most important skills they need to know—how to facilitate a constructive coaching conversation. It's amazing. People wonder why most teams are so dysfunctional. It's pretty simple: There's no coach! How in the hell can you expect managers to coach and develop their teams when *they* haven't ever received any coaching?"

Brad nodded. "Good point. At least that makes me feel a *little* better."

Coach cracked open another peanut and waited patiently for Brad's next question.

"Okay, so let me ask you something else," Brad said. "Based on your experience, what would you say is the single most important thing I need to know about becoming a world-class leader?"

"Simple," Coach said without hesitation. "At its core, leadership isn't a head issue; it's a heart issue. Most managers today have it all wrong. They're so wrapped up in their damn spreadsheets, PowerPoint presentations, and Six Sigma BS that somewhere along the line they forgot these aren't machines we're dealing with—they're people. They don't realize that as a coach, the more you give, the more you'll get. The more you care, the more they'll contribute."

Coach paused to take a sip from his pint and then added, "If you want really want to become a world-class leader, here's my advice: Get your heart right first, and your head will follow."

Brad was furiously taking notes, trying to capture what he was hearing and process it so he could ask follow-up questions.

"Okay, I hear what you're saying, but if my role as a coach is to constantly observe, evaluate, and coach my team," he said, "don't tactics and strategies—or, as you put it, 'head issues'—play an important part in that process?"

"Absolutely. Listen, I'm not saying that it's not important to teach your people the fundamentals. It is. It just shouldn't be your very first priority. You've got to understand that change cannot be imposed; it must be chosen. In order to get people to improve, they first have to *want* to improve."

Coach pointed toward a nearby television that was playing one of the great European Champion's League soccer matchups—Manchester United against Bayern Munich. He then asked, "You've heard of Sir Alex Furgeson, haven't you?

Brad shot back, "Come on—do you think I'm a stupid American or something? Of course I've heard

*As a coach the more you give,
the more you'll get. The more you care,
the more they'll contribute.*

of him. He's a legend—the most successful manager in British football history." He paused for a moment before adding, "Even though he's the nemesis of my boys in blue, Chelsea."

Coach replied, "Yeah, well when Sir Alex first arrived at MAN U, they hadn't won an English title in *twenty years*; again they found themselves in the relegation zone. Do you have any idea how he turned things around so quickly and transformed that club into one of history's most successful sports franchises?"

"No," Brad answered, "but I'm guessing that drafting David Beckham and Ryan Giggs probably didn't hurt."

"Correction," Coach responded. "He didn't *draft* Giggs and Beckham—he *developed* them."

Brad sat there with a confused look on his face. "What do you mean?"

Coach continued, "Like most companies today, your boy José Mourinho and his Russian Oligarch boss built their strategy around on spending boatloads of money to *acquire* talent. Sir Alex, on the other hand, focused on *developing* it."

Brad jokingly replied, "Watch it . . ."

"Back in the late eighties and early nineties, when Sir Alex was implementing his long-term strategy to ensure that MAN U was consistently at the top of the table, the foundation of his master plan was based on creating a youth-development academy where he found young teenage lads like Giggs, Beckham, and Scholes and coached them into world champions," Coach explained.

"So, how did he do that?" Brad asked.

Coach replied, "Well, for starters he constantly communicated the four most powerful words any coach or leader can say: *I believe in you.*" Coach paused, but not long enough for Brad to pepper him with another question. "I want you to remember something: Behind every great player is a coach who believed in that player more than the player believed in himself."

Coach was on a roll now. As Brad wrote his notes, he did his best to maintain some eye contact.

"Over the years," Coach went on. "I've coached some amazing people who have gone on to achieve some extraordinary things. And I see every bit as much potential in you as I did in them. But here's the catch: You must realize that as a coach the only way you can achieve your potential is to first help your team members achieve theirs."

"So how do I help my team members achieve their potential?

"That's where the system comes in," Coach said as he looked at his watch and shot a glance in the direction of

Behind every great player is a coach who believed in that player more than the player believed in himself.

the crew who had gathered by the pool table. "But, unfortunately, it looks like our time for this evening is up."

"Are you serious?" Brad nearly screamed. "You're killing me! Can you at least give me a hint?"

"Nope," Coach said with a smirk. "But I can give you some more homework. I want you to think about the three toughest challenges you're facing right now in trying to get the most out of your team. Give it some thought, make some notes, and we'll reconvene next Friday. Same time, same place. Oh, and don't be late."

Please note: if you'd like to go deeper, I've created an exclusive FREE video training series you definitely won't want to miss. For instant access, register now at ProductivityDrivers.com/WCCInsiders/

• • •

The next day Brad returned from his morning jog, pulled a bottle of water from his refrigerator, and sat down on his leather couch to review his notes from the previous evening's coaching conversation while he watched Sportscenter. With a yellow highlighter, he began to mark some key coaching points:

- *The secret is all in the approach. Stop acting like a manager and start acting like a coach.*
- *The first step to becoming a world-class leader is to realize that the rules of the game have changed—and so, too, must you.*
- *Great coaches consistently get the most out of their people because they consistently put the most into their people.*
- *As a coach, the more you give, the more you'll get. The more you care, the more they'll contribute.*
- *Behind every great player is a coach who believed in that player more than the player believed in himself.*
- *As a coach, the only way you can achieve your potential is to first help your team members achieve theirs.*
- *Coaching is not merely something that you, as a manager, must do. A coach is someone that you, as a leader, must become.*
- *When all is said and done and we've completed this journey we call life, what will matter most is not what we have achieved—but rather who we have become.*

As a coach, the only way you can achieve your potential is to first help your team members achieve theirs.

Magic Pint Glass

The following Friday, Brad zipped into the lot at Halftime, parked his car in the first space he could find, and jogged toward the front door.

It was 5:41 p.m., and he was late.

He looked to the back of the bar and saw Coach sitting there—reading glasses on the tip of his nose—drawing something on the back of a cocktail napkin.

Barely acknowledging the others in the bar, Brad made a beeline back to Coach's Corner, his apology already prepared in his mind.

"Sales Manager, you're late," Coach grumbled, beating Brad to the punch.

"I know, Coach. My bad. Today was the last day I could get fitted for my tux and to get it back in time for next Friday's big awards shindig."

"Tux?" Coach raised an eyebrow. "You going to the

Oscars or somethin'? Well, have you written your acceptance speech yet?"

"No, but I have jotted down a few ideas," Brad said before he realized that Coach had been joking about the speech. "I mean," he continued, "I don't want to go up there looking like an idiot in front of five hundred of the company's top brass, right? They might have second thoughts and take back the award!"

Coach just shook his head. "So did you do your homework?"

Brad nodded as he held up his journal.

"In case I forgot to mention it, the penalty for not showing up on time to one of my coaching conversations is a pint for every minute you're late," he said. "But since I'm in an especially good mood today because my Packers made the playoffs again, I'm going to give you a chance to get off the hook. I'll make you a bet. If I'm able to guess at least two out of the three biggest challenges you're having with improving your team's productivity, then you buy the next round and we'll call it even. Anything less and it's on me."

"Done." Brad said. "A chance at free tuition? I'm in!"

Coach hunched over the table and started rubbing his pint glass as if it were some sort of magic crystal ball. "I see Es—three of them, in fact. The first problem has to do with a lack of Efficiency," he said. "It seems that most of your team members are working hard, but they're working on the wrong things. There's a lot of input (activity) but very little output (results). In fact, they're so busy *reacting* instead of *acting* that they never really get anything done."

"That's pretty darn impressive, old man."

Coach resumed his fortune-telling position and rubbed his pint glass again. "The second E has to do with Effort—or rather, a lack of it. It seems that others on your team are coming into work and just going through the motions—doing just enough to get by. It's as if you're only getting 150 horses out of a 350-horsepower engine. Right?"

"Dang, you're good! How'd you know that?" Brad asked.

"That's two for two," Coach said. "Do you want to go double or nothing and throw in a plate of nachos for good measure?"

"Bring it," Brad shot back. "But I guarantee you'll never get this one."

Coach rubbed his magic pint for the third and final time. "Okay, it looks like the last E stands for . . . oh, yes . . . Effectiveness," he said. "Your salespeople may be making calls and attending meetings, but they're unsure of the next step they should be close for and are getting lost in the sales process. Oh, and when it comes to getting them to input their data into the CRM system, forget about it. It's like trying to pull a pint of Guinness from an Irishman's hands!"

"Wrong!" Brad shouted.

Coach stared back in disbelief. "Really?" he said. "You're kiddin' me. What's the third one?"

Brad laughed. "Getting them to actually show up and have a pint with me so I don't have to sit there celebrating all by myself, looking like a complete jackass!"

"I'll tell you what," Coach said when he stopped laughing. "I'll cut you a break on the nachos. But while you're up, go ahead and grab one for yourself, too."

As Brad left for the bar, Coach began scribbling on the chalkboard. He wrote,

$$\text{Employee Productivity} = \text{Efficiency} \times \text{Effort} \times \text{Effectiveness}$$

When Brad returned with their drinks, he stopped and stared at the chalkboard.

"Hey, wait a minute," he said as he placed the pints on the table. "I was told there'd be no math in this class. Did you forget? I'm a sales guy—not an engineer. The only numbers I pay attention to follow dollar signs."

"Okay, Mr. Sales Guy, do you want to learn how to

solve some of the problems we were just talking about?" Coach said.

"Absolutely."

Coach drew a division line under the equation. Below it he wrote a question mark. "It's simple. Figure out the common denominator, and you'll solve the problem."

Brad just sat there quietly with a puzzled look on his face.

Sensing Brad's confusion, Coach glanced around the bar. When he found what he'd been searching for, he pointed to the wall behind one of the pool tables.

"Here's a hint," he said. "Go take a look at that picture over there next to the dartboard—the one behind that pool table over there—and tell me what you see."

Brad walked over, stood about ten feet in front of the picture, and slowly but loudly began to read, "We . . . proudly . . . serve . . . Stroh's . . ."

Coach got up and walked over to Brad and laughed. "No—take a closer look."

Brad walked a few steps closer.

"*Now* what do you see?" Coach asked.

Brad looked past the beer-marketing slogan and saw his reflection on the picture's surface.

"*Me?*" he said. "You think *I'm* the solution? Are you serious? Our senior leaders haven't even been able to figure it out, and you think *I* can?"

"I can guarantee you one thing: They've never tried what I'm about to teach you. You see, they don't realize that the fundamental problem is not a frontline employee *skillset* issue—it's a frontline employee *behavioral* issue. And the *real* reason most employees aren't doing what they're supposed to be doing actually has a lot less to do with the employees themselves and a lot more to do with their managers."

"I'm not sure I follow," Brad admitted as they headed back to Coach's Corner.

"You see, most organizational leaders don't realize that the main reason employees are underperforming is the same reason why most training initiatives fail to stick. It's the same reason why it's so difficult to get bottom-up buy-in on strategic change initiatives. The main reason is a lack of management reinforcement—*especially* at the frontline manager level," Coach said he slipped back into the booth.

"Okay, now you've really lost me."

"Think of it this way," said Coach, after pausing for a moment. "In football you can draw up a beautiful game plan and have a killer playbook, but if your quarterback can't command the huddle on the field, your team will fail to execute the plays."

As Brad took a seat across from him, Coach leaned forward and pointed at Brad's chest. "As a frontline manager, you, my friend, are like the quarterback on the field. Do you want to solve the problems we've been talking about and get your team members to bring their A-game each and every day? Do you want to take your team's performance—and your career—to the next level?"

Brad nodded.

Coach flipped over the cocktail napkin. "Here's how you do it," he said.

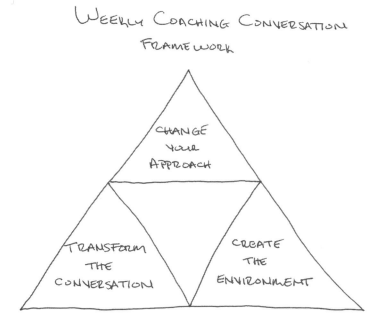

Mindset

B rad silently stared at the cocktail napkin as if it had some sort of mystical power. There it was in illustration form, scribbled on the back of a two-ply paper napkin with *Budweiser* stamped on the other side. Brad's eyes were fixed on it with anticipation. Surely it would stand on the table and begin speaking with the voice of James Earl Jones. Or perhaps sparks would fly from the edges as Coach levitated to some point just above the table. Or perhaps a video would begin playing inside the napkin, like a message from Princess Leia to young Luke Skywalker.

A few seconds passed, and the napkin didn't come to life after all. Brad looked up at Coach with a puzzled look as if it say, *Is* this *it? Really?*

"One thing you'll learn when you have as many gray hairs as I do is that the probability of a plan succeeding is in direct proportion to its simplicity. Don't get fancy.

Keep it simple. It doesn't matter if we're talking about marketing, customer service, operations, engineering, finance, sales, IT, or HR—this framework flat-out works. And the reason why it works is because it's simple to understand, easy to apply, and delivers results. Oh, and your team will absolutely love it."

"You're selling me pretty hard on this system, aren't you?"

"I don't have to sell it, son," Coach shot back, motioning toward the back of the room where a number of successful executives from Coach's crew had already gathered. "The results speak for themselves."

"Touché."

Having made his point, Coach continued, "Look, there is a lot you need to learn about becoming a world-class coach, and it's going to take time. But having been in this game as long as I have, I can guarantee you that the single most important skill you must master if you want to consistently get the most out of your team and *systematically* improve their performance is by facilitating what I call *a weekly coaching conversation*." Coach paused for a moment before adding, "And since you're in sales, the objective of the weekly coaching conversation is to transform your one-on-ones from an interrogation of the pipeline into a constructive coaching conversation."

"Okay, I'm listening."

"However, before you're even ready to sit down with your team members and start having your weekly coaching conversations, there's some important prep work that needs to be done. So let's get to it. You ready?"

Brad gave an enthusiastic nod, and Coach launched into the framework, shifting his verbal intensity into high gear.

"Step One: Change Your Approach," Coach announced.

"We touched on this earlier, but I want to reiterate a few key points," he said. "The difference that makes the difference is all in the approach. Stop acting like a manager; start acting like a coach. You need to redefine what you perceive your role to be. You've got to get it into your head and heart what your *real* job is: to pull every ounce of potential from each and every team member each and every day. Got it?"

"Got it," Brad said as he scribbled some notes.

"They are your team, and you are their coach. What they may or may not be able to achieve is a direct reflection of you and your approach. No excuses. Their problems are your problems. Their victories are your victories. And their failures are your failures. Are you with me?"

"Yep," Brad said without even looking up. He was still frantically taking notes, trying to capture every word Coach uttered.

*As a coach your job is to pull
every ounce of potential from each and
every team member each and
every day.*

"Good. Now make a note: How you define success will ultimately determine the level to which you succeed."

Brad slammed his pen down on the table and looked up. "Okay, now you've lost me."

"Let me show you what I mean." Coach grabbed a peanut and handed it to Brad. "Here, see if you can throw this peanut into that garbage can right there."

Brad took the peanut and tossed it into the can, which was only a few feet away.

"Did you succeed?" Coach asked.

"Of course. I'm one-for-one, aren't I?"

Coach handed him another peanut. "Go ahead and give it another shot, but this time go for that garbage can way over there." The can he pointed to was about twenty feet across the room.

Brad took aim as if he were shooting a three-pointer and tossed the peanut. It came within an inch of hitting a Stanford coed in the head before landing on the floor a few inches away from his target.

Coach said, "What about now? Do you still think you're successful?"

"Come on," the manager said. "Fifty percent might be good enough for some slackers, but it sure as heck isn't good enough for me."

Coach could tell by Brad's voice that he was joking, but he was never one to let a coachable moment slip by.

"Interesting," he said to himself.

"What?"

"Interesting," Coach repeated.

"What!"

Coach turned his attention back to Brad. "I just find it interesting that you're not satisfied with a 50 percent success rate throwing peanuts into a garbage can," he said. "Yet when only 50 percent of your team members make their number, you want to celebrate because you're Sales Leader of the Year."

"Ouch," Brad said. "That's a low blow, Coach. But go ahead and bring it. I can take it."

Coach smiled. "Atta boy. Moving on, make a note: What you believe affects what they achieve and you receive."

"Come again?"

"What you do is controlled by how you think—your mindset." Coach explained. "Your mindset is basically made up of a series of beliefs and associations that control how you think and, ultimately, how you behave. For example, let's say that one of your core beliefs is that winners are born—not made. In other words, what if you believed that trying to coach, develop, and improve your team's performance was a complete waste of time?

What you believe affects
what they achieve and you receive.

How might this mindset affect your priorities—what you choose to focus on?"

After thinking for a moment, Brad replied, "I obviously wouldn't waste much time trying to coach or develop my team members. I'd probably just leave that up to HR."

"Exactly. Now just imagine for a moment if a professional coach had this same mindset. After drafting a bunch of young players, he sat them down and said, 'Gentlemen, I believe you either got it or you ain't got it. So me and the other coaches ain't gonna bother making you practice and trying to improve your performance, because we all know that's a complete waste of time.'"

Brad couldn't help but laugh out loud at how absurd this sounded.

"Seriously, what if a professional coach had this mindset?" Coach continued. "What if he believed that after draft day his job was more or less done, and all he needed to do was given them their comp plan, put them through training a few days a year, and then show up for game day? How might this coach's mindset affect the likelihood that he would be able to get the most out of his players? How might this coach's mindset impact the probability that his team could compete and win at the highest level?"

"Wow," said Brad, "I guess I'm really starting to see that the connection between the approach of a professional sports coach and this new management approach you're talking about is very similar."

Coach continued, "Yep, now make a note: Mind your mind. It all starts with you and your mindset. Change your mindset, and you'll change your behavior. Change your behavior, and you'll change their behavior. Change their behavior, and you'll change their performance. It's that simple. So before you waste all this time and energy trying to change your team's behavior, take a good long look in the mirror and first focus on what *you* need to change. It all starts with you, my friend. You are the catalyst. Remember, nothing changes unless you do."

It all starts with you and your mindset. Change your mindset, and you'll change your behavior. Change your behavior, and you'll change their behavior. Change their behavior, and you'll change their performance.

The Talk

Little Nikki set a plate of nachos on the table in front of Coach and put a smaller, empty plate in front of Brad.

"Extra jalapeños, just like you like 'em, Coach," he said with a smile.

"Perfect!" Coach said as he slid the plate closer to Brad.

While Little Nikki returned to the bar, Brad stuffed his face and mumbled, "Step one, change your approach. Stop acting like a manager and start acting like a coach. Got it. What's next?"

Coach passed Brad a napkin and shook his head.

"Step Two: Create the Environment. Or, to put it another way," Coach said, "you've got to pull the weeds before you plant the seeds."

"Create what?" Brad asked as he washed down a jalapeño with a swig of Pilsner.

"Let me give you a quick example," Coach continued.

"Early in Vince Lombardi's football coaching career, the bulk of his experience was as the head coach for a small, private high school—St. Cecilia's. While Lombardi was at St. Cecilia's, he won six straight parochial school state titles and at one point won thirty-two consecutive games. So when he finally landed a position in the pros as the offensive coordinator for the New York Giants, he figured he'd just use the exact same system—the same approach—he had used in his winning career at St. Cecilia's."

As an avid sports fan, Brad knew all about Coach Lombardi's legendary success as the head coach of the NFL's Green Bay Packers. "Well, it obviously worked, right?" asked Brad. "I mean, he's one of the greatest football coaches of all time."

"Nope," Coach said. "In fact, every time Lombardi tried to have a coaching conversation with one of his team members, they'd tune him out and wouldn't listen. In fact, the players even mocked him for treating them like they were a bunch of high school kids. One day Lombardi had finally had enough. He decided to talk to Frank Gifford, the team leader and star player at the time. After finding Frank in the locker room playing cards with a couple of other team veterans, Lombardi approached them with complete humility and said, 'Guys—what the hell am I doing wrong?'

"And with that," Coach continued, "everything changed.

You see, Lombardi learned a valuable lesson that day: To get your team to become coachable, *you* must first become coachable. To get your team to open up, *you* must first open up. To get your team to embrace constructive coaching and developmental feedback, *you* must first embrace constructive coaching and developmental feedback. As a coach, you set the standard for your team to follow. And your personal example is the most powerful leadership tool you have."

Brad did his best to capture all of Coach's insights in his journal. There was a pause in the conversation as Brad tapped his pen on the table and reviewed his notes while Coach enjoyed a few nachos.

"That makes sense," Brad said, "but what's that got to do with what you said a minute ago—something about pulling the weeds before you plant the seeds?"

Coach slapped the table and reached for his pint.

"Every time I talk about Coach Lombardi, God rest his soul, I get all fired up," he said, washing down the last of the nachos on his plate. "Lombardi learned to plant seeds and help them grow. When we talk about the process of becoming a coach and consistently getting the most out of your team, what we're really talking about is planting seeds in the minds of your team—seeds of self-confidence; seeds of belief, desire, positive expectation; and, ultimately, seeds of greatness."

To get your team to become coachable, you must first become coachable. To get your team to open up, you must first open up. To get your team to embrace constructive coaching and developmental feedback, you must first embrace constructive coaching and developmental feedback. As a coach, you set the standard for your team to follow. And your personal example is the most powerful leadership tool you have.

Coach paused to search for an analogy.

"A farmer hoping to reap a huge harvest," he continued, "wouldn't just walk up to any old dry, unfertile patch of dirt choked with weeds and start tossing out seeds like they were chicken feed, would he?" To punctuate the point, Coach threw a handful of peanuts across the floor.

"Nope."

"Why not?"

"Because if you don't properly prepare the soil," Brad said, "the seeds won't take root. And if the field is already choked with weeds, the seeds will never stand a chance."

"Exactly," Coach said. "Make a note: Pull the weeds before you plant the seeds."

Brad's journal again became the focus of attention.

"Okay, let me put it this way," Coach added. "You need to hit the rest button on your relationship with your team. You need to sit down with each team member and have a heart-to-heart to see where you stand. You need to identify and remove the friction points in your relationship that could be preventing your team members from being open to having a coaching conversation. Just like Coach Lombardi, you've got to be the first one to put your cards on the table and ask, 'What am *I* doing wrong? What can *I* do better? How can *I* improve?'"

"Well, *that's* going to be a lot of fun," Brad sarcastically moaned.

"Just remember, when they start opening up and telling you some things you'd probably rather not hear, don't get defensive. Don't judge—just listen. Really try to understand their perspective and see things through their eyes. Try to understand their perception of you and your management approach, because you know what?"

"What?"

"*Their* perception is *your* reality. Make a note: Leadership is a reciprocal process. In order for people to follow you, they must trust and believe in you. And in order for them to trust and believe in you, you must first trust and believe in them. Trust is the foundation of leadership, and it's at the core of becoming a world-class coach."

Brad, still taking notes, didn't look up as he asked his next question. "Okay, so I sit down with each team member and ask what I'm doing wrong—or, better yet, what I can improve on," he said. "And after they proceed to unload on me—telling me what a selfish jerk I've been—then what?"

"Simple," Coach said. "Apologize. But don't just say it; *mean* it. Look them in the eyes and tell them the truth. Tell them exactly what you've shared with me over these past couple of weeks. And then, most important, *change your*

Leadership is a reciprocal process. In order for people to follow you, they must trust and believe in you. And in order for them to trust and believe in you, you must first trust and believe in them.

approach. Stop acting like a manager and start acting like a coach!"

Brad took a deep breath. "Okay," he said, "so once I've pulled the weeds, then I start planting the seeds, right?"

"Wrong."

"Wrong?"

"Dang, son, didn't your mama teach you anything about gardening? You can't treat different seeds the same and expect them all to flourish, now can you? The next thing you've got to do is figure out which types of seeds grow best under which conditions."

Coach pointed toward a line of old framed photos hanging on a nearby wall. Among the black-and-white mug shots of famous athletes and celebrities hung a picture of a racehorse, and Coach was pointing right at it.

"Ever see the movie *Seabiscuit*?" Coach asked.

"Great movie," Brad responded. "One of my favorites. Right up there with *Caddy Shack* and *The Hangover*. I must have seen it a dozen times."

"Remember how, early on, Seabiscuit had a legendary trainer by the name of Fitzsimmons? If you'll recall, Fitzsimmons saw a lot of potential in Seabiscuit, but for some reason the horse just wasn't performing up to expectations. Fitzsimmons thought the horse was just too darn lazy. So do you remember what he did?"

"Yeah, he tried to break him down and beat it out of him," Brad recalled.

"And did it work?" Coach asked.

"Nope," Brad said. "I think he either finished dead last or in the back of the pack in his first ten races."

"Right. So then along comes Seabiscuit's new trainer— an old, washed up horse-whisperer by the name of Tom Smith. And lo and behold, Seabiscuit starts winning every race, eventually becoming the number-one racehorse in the whole damn country! Same horse. Same potential. But *vastly* different results."

Coach paused for a minute, letting his point sink in. "Let me ask you this: What made the difference? Was it the horse or the trainer?"

"The trainer," Brad answered without even thinking twice. "Seabiscuit had it in him the whole time."

"So what did Smith know that Fitzsimmons didn't?"

"Simple: He knew his horse."

"Exactly!" Coach said in a booming voice. "Make a note: Get to know your people. If you want them to trust you, you've got to earn it. You've got to make it a top priority to continually invest in those relationships before they'll start to pay dividends. Find out what's special and unique about each of your team members. Learn about their backgrounds, their upbringings, their idiosyncrasies, their strengths, their weaknesses, their hopes, their dreams, and their desires. Find out what drives them. Not only will this help you establish a higher degree of trust and rapport with your team, but it will also give you vital information that you're going to use during your weekly coaching conversations. Are you following me?"

"Absolutely! This is great stuff," Brad said as he finished jotting down his notes. "But I have a question. Going back to what you were talking about earlier, how will I know when it's time to start planting the seeds? At this point I don't think my team will even be receptive to having a coaching conversation. When will I know I've developed enough trust and rapport so that they'll be open to having these weekly coaching conversations?"

"Don't worry," said Coach. "You'll know. Trust me. You'll know."

The Greatest Gift

Coach returned with another round of drinks and looked over Brad's notes as he settled back into his seat.

"You're catching on, Sales Manager," he said. "Had enough, or do you think you can handle more?" Coach pulled out his journal, wrote something down, and returned his attention to his newest protégé.

"I can handle it," said Brad.

"Excellent!" Coach replied. "While the framework is universal and works for any manager, since you're in sales, let me ask you a question." After pausing, he asked Brad, "What's the greatest gift you can give a salesperson?"

"A bluebird deal," Brad shot back.

"Wrong."

"A great territory."

"Nope."

"A hot wife . . . a fancy car . . . I don't know!"

Coach laughed. "All right, all right," he said. "Let me help you out. The greatest gift you can give a salesperson— or any person, for that matter—is self-confidence." He scooped a handful of peanuts from the bowl between them and continued. "As a salesperson, the first sales job is always on yourself. It doesn't matter how great your pitch is, how good your closing skills are, or how pretty that PowerPoint presentation might be—if the prospect can sense that you don't believe in yourself and what you're selling, the prospect ain't gonna buy. It's that simple."

Coach continued. "In order to convince, *you* must first be convinced. Not only must you have confidence in your product and your company, but more importantly, you must have confidence in *yourself*. It doesn't matter whether you're in marketing, operations, engineering, finance, accounting, customer service, IT, or HR—the same principle applies. Improving your team member's self-confidence is the first step to improving his or her performance."

"Great stuff," Brad said as he continued taking notes. "Great stuff."

"No need to kiss my a--," Coach said with a grin. "We talked about how it's your job to believe in your people more than they believe in themselves. Remember?"

Brad nodded.

"Well, the next step is to transfer that belief—that

sense of confidence—to your team. After you've raised *your* performance standards and expectations, you've got to get them to raise *theirs*. You've got to get them to believe that they haven't even scratched the surface of their potential, and that—with the right coaching—they're capable of performing at a much higher level."

Brad put his pen down and looked at Coach. "How am I supposed to do *that?*"

Coach stared across the table deep in thought.

"Okay, let me ask you another question," Coach said. "Why do you think professional coaches are so obsessed with watching game film?"

"Well, they watch game film to break down each player's performance," Brad answered. "To figure out what each player did right and what he did wrong so they can help them improve next time."

"And once the coaches have broken down each team member's performance and pinpointed what they need to work on in order to improve, what do they do with that information?" Coach asked. "Do they run up to HR asking for a performance evaluation sheet, write down what each team member needs to work on in order to improve, seal it up, and file it away until the end-of-year performance reviews?"

Brad laughed out loud at how absurd this sounded.

"No! They use the info to give their team members immediate feedback so they can improve in the very next game."

"Feedback! Yes, lad, that's it! People need feedback and coaching to improve their performance, don't they? If your team doesn't know what they're doing right and what they're doing wrong, how can they adjust? How can they improve?"

Coach leaned forward. "Make a note: The only way to *systematically* improve performance is through consistently giving constructive coaching and developmental feedback. And in the business world, just like in sports, there's a direct correlation between the quantity and quality of coaching a person receives and his or her level of performance improvement."

Coach took out his pen, grabbed a cocktail napkin, and drew a chart. Pointing to the chart, he said, "In other words, a lot of coaching . . . a lot of improvement. A little coaching . . . a little improvement. No coaching . . . no improvement."

"That seems pretty obvious."

"You'd think so, wouldn't you?" Coach rhetorically asked. "The sad truth is that most managers aren't giving their team members *any* constructive coaching or developmental feedback.

"Speaking of which," Coach continued, "I'm curious.

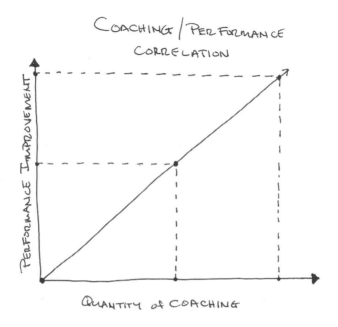

COACHING / PERFORMANCE CORRELATION

QUANTITY of COACHING

How often are you giving your team members constructive coaching and developmental feedback?"

Brad took a moment to think that over. "Well, I don't know how 'constructive' or 'developmental' it is, but I guess I at least give them feedback once a year during their annual performance reviews."

Coach shook his head. "Once a year? You think coaching your team *once a year* is going to have *any* impact on improving their performance?"

"Well, since you put it that way, probably not," Brad said, "but isn't that pretty standard these days for most companies?"

Coach sighed. "Yeah, it's pretty standard—and pretty pathetic. Employers wonder why employees are so disengaged, unmotivated, and underperforming. Think of it this way. If you have a *weekly* coaching conversation with your team members, you're giving them *fifty times* more opportunities to improve their performance than the competition is getting. And a side benefit is that the built-in weekly cadence will also help you improve your team's accountability and give you a consistent venue to look for those coachable moments."

Brad began writing. "Coachable moments?" he asked.

"I've got another Lombardi story to illustrate my point," Coach said. "You love my Packer stories, don't you?"

"No; actually, I'm a Dallas Cowboys fan."

Coach shook his head. "Figures. Anyway, Jerry Kramer, one of the offensive linemen on Coach Lombardi's team, told a story about what happened when he jumped offside once in a scrimmage. Lombardi immediately got in his face and yelled at the top of his lungs, "The concentration period of a college student is five minutes, a high school student is three minutes, and a kindergartener is thirty seconds—and you don't even have that! So where does that put *you*?' After practice, Kramer went back into the locker room thinking, *there's not a chance in hell I'm ever going to play for this guy again.* Then all of a sudden Lombardi burst through the door, headed straight over to Kramer, bent down, looked him dead in the eye, patted him on the back, and said, 'Son, one of these days you're going to be the best damn guard in football.' With that he abruptly walked away. Kramer later said that moment was the turning point in his career. From that day on, he poured his heart out for Coach Lombardi because he knew Lombardi believed in him—and he didn't want to let him down. And you know what?"

"What?"

"He didn't. Jerry Kramer became one of the thirteen players on a losing 1–10–1 team that Lombardi inherited back in '59 who either became an All Pro or a Hall of Fame player. You see, unlike most managers today, Lombardi didn't complain about the talent that *wasn't* there— he focused on developing the talent that *was*."

Coach again fixed his gaze on Brad. "Same player. Same team. Same potential. But *vastly* different results. So, what was the difference—the player or the coach?"

"It was obviously the coach—but to be more specific, it was the coach's *approach*," Brad said.

"Bingo," Coach said. "Make a note: As a coach, everything you do and everything you say sends a message to your team. The question you've got to constantly ask yourself is this: What message am I sending? And always remember: What you say affects how they play."

The only way to systematically improve performance is through consistently giving constructive coaching and developmental feedback.

The Coaching
Conversation Continues

B rad looked up from his journal, a puzzled expres-
sion on his face. "I get what you're saying about
the importance of having a weekly coaching conversation, and I get that what I say affects how my team
plays. But my question is, *what do I say?*"

Coach smiled. "Good question. Let's start by analyzing
what your current one-on-ones look like."

"Well, for starters, there's really no set cadence and
no consistent process. I guess I just kinda wing it," Brad
said.

Shaking his head, Coach asked, "How can you expect
to get consistent results from an inconsistent process?
Anyway, grab your pen and journal and get ready, because we're going to kick it up a notch. As you can see,"

he said, gesturing toward the back of the bar, "the crew is getting restless."

Brad looked toward the pool tables, where a crowd of corporate executive types were partying like college kids, singing and dancing.

Coach jumped up, grabbed a piece of chalk, and started scribbling something on the chalkboard behind the table. He wrote:

1. Stop focusing so much on the prize that you forget about the process.

Coach put down the chalk and asked, "Why is it that most people come to work Monday morning with the best intentions to get a lot done, but at the end of the day have so little to show for their efforts?"

Brad shrugged. "I dunno."

"Let me give you a hint," Coach said. "Think back to your issue with your team not working as *efficiently* as they should be."

From the look on Brad's face, it was obvious he was drawing a blank.

Coach peered over the rim of his glasses and continued.

"Still don't know? What if I told you that you are part of the problem?"

"*Me?*" said Brad, oozing with sarcasm. "Not a chance! I'm the cocky guy who's got this management stuff all figured out. Remember?"

Coach smiled in recognition of his protégé's newfound sense of humility.

"I want you to remember three important things. First, you've got to help your team members minimize distractions and maximize focus on *weekly* priorities. Second, you need to stop focusing so much on the prize that you forget about the process. And finally, you've got to understand that what gets reinforced gets done. Focus controls behavior. Questions control focus. If you as a manager are not *knowingly* asking the right questions, there's a good chance that you're *unknowingly* reinforcing the wrong behaviors."

"Whew!" Brad said, wiping his brow. "Where'd you learn all this stuff? You sure as heck didn't pick it up on the football field."

"No, I learned it while studying behavioral psychology," Coach said, "but that's beside the point. When you sit down with your team for your weekly one-on-ones, what type of questions are you asking?"

Brad half-jokingly replied, "I'm all about *Glengary Glen Ross. A–B–C. Always. Be. Closing.* So of course I ask the same two questions that every other sales manager asks: How big's the deal? And when is it closing?"

Coach shook his head and sighed. "Well, that explains it."

"Explains what?"

"Why you can't get your salespeople to do more prospecting." Coach grabbed another cocktail napkin and drew a sales funnel diagram on the back. At the top he wrote *All Prospects* and at the bottom he wrote *Closed Deals.*

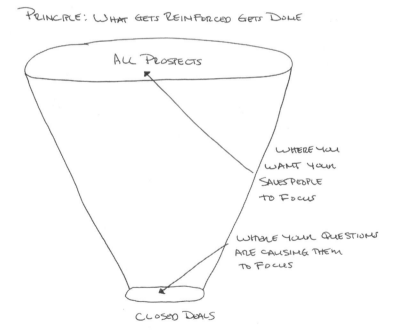

Coach tapped on the drawing with his pen and said, "When you ask those questions—'How big is the deal?' and 'When is it closing?'—where on the sales funnel does that put the focus?"

"On the bottom."

"If you want them to start doing more prospecting on a more consistent basis," Coach continued, "where on the sales funnel *should* you be focusing their attention?"

"On the top."

"Are you starting to see the problem here?"

"*Now* I get what you're saying. You bring up a good point. I guess I never realized how much of an impact what *I* do affects what *they* do."

Coach just smiled. "Remember: A skilled coach uses Socratic questioning to control focus and direct behavior in order to initiate learning and improve performance."

When Brad finished writing his notes, Coach wrote the second key point on the chalkboard:

2. Don't just celebrate the touchdowns— celebrate the first downs.

"You said that some members of your team weren't putting forth the extra effort. You said they seemed to be

Don't just celebrate the touchdowns—
celebrate the first downs.

just going through the motions—doing just enough to skate by. What if I told you that you were part of this problem too?"

Brad frowned. "Hey, wait a minute. I'm starting to see a theme here. What the heck is this? Beat-up-on-Brad day?"

Coach smiled. "Relax. While you may be part of the problem, you're going to be an even bigger part of the solution. Just do what I say and you'll be a hero. I promise."

"So what does my team's sub-par performance have to do with celebrating first downs?" Brad asked.

"Make a note," Coach said. "Long-term success requires short-term focus. And the fastest way to improve performance is to help your team members set process-oriented, weekly goals and then positively reinforce small, incremental improvements. This isn't some management gimmick; it's a scientific fact," Coach continued. "What gets reinforced gets done. Whether we're talking about succeeding in business, sports, teaching, or even parenting, the same timeless principles apply. The goal here is steady, consistent progress—day in and day out. All you're trying to do is to get your team members to be a little better today than they were yesterday."

Back at the board, Coach wrote his third key point:

Embrace mistakes as coachable moments.

"This one has to do with some of the challenges your team is having around *effectiveness*—or skill competency level—"

"Wait a minute, wait a minute," Brad interrupted. "Let me guess. This one's my fault too."

"Actually, no," Coach said. "Chalk this one up to conventional wisdom not being all that wise. For some reason, conventional wisdom has always been that it was the primary responsibility of HR to train and develop *your* team. It's not. They obviously play an important part, but ultimately, that's *your* job. In fact, that's one of the most important aspects of your job and why it's so critical that you—and your company's leaders—redefine your role.

"The best way to systematically improve employee performance is by giving them constructive coaching and developmental feedback on a *weekly* basis. That's why the weekly coaching conversation is so important. And, frankly, without this critical piece of the puzzle in place, trying to do *any* training for frontline employees is a colossal waste of time, energy, and money because it won't stick."

Brad nodded and continued taking notes while Coach took a sip from his pint.

Embrace mistakes as coachable moments.

"Building a high-performance team can be achieved only through the identification and perfection of seemingly small things consistently done right over time. But here's the catch: We learn far more from our mistakes than we do from our successes," Coach continued. "If you only give your team members positive reinforcement, they may feel all warm and fuzzy, but they're never going to improve. You've got to push them and challenge them if you want them to grow. You've got to accept that failure is a natural byproduct of success."

Brad kept frantically scribbling down notes, trying to capture every word.

"Keep in mind, your job is to evaluate, not judge; it's to coach, not criticize," Coach added. "Learn to embrace mistakes as coachable moments. View them as opportunities for improvement. As long as you've done a good job of creating—and maintaining—an environment that's conducive to coaching, your team members will not only be *open* to having a coaching conversation, they'll proactively come to you *asking* for it."

Just as Coach was about to start explaining the importance of the five critical coaching questions, the buzzing of his phone cut him off. He pulled the phone from his pocket and looked at the number on the screen.

"Gimme a sec," Coach said. "I need to take this call."

He stepped away from the table, giving Brad a few minutes to collect his thoughts and go over his notes.

"Everything okay?" Brad asked when Coach returned a few minutes later.

"I hate to do this, but I've got to cut this coaching conversation a little short. I have to catch the next flight to Europe for an emergency board meeting."

Brad had begun to see Coach as larger than life, but a spur-of-the-moment business trip to Europe still stunned him a bit.

"Really?" he asked.

"Yeah, one of the companies I'm an active board member for is trying to close an M&A deal they've been working on for months. I'll probably be gone for a week or so."

Brad noticed that Coach's tone was casual, as if the trip were as routine as a drive around the block.

"I'm sorry I won't be here next Friday to celebrate after you receive your big award," Coach said.

"Ah, no worries," said Brad, doing his best to mask his disappointment.

Coach slapped Brad on the back with his left hand and extended an envelope in his right hand. "I got you a little something," he said, "but don't open it until right before the awards banquet."

Brad flipped the envelope over a few times, resisting the

temptation to slice it open and examine what was inside. As Coach made his way toward the exit, yelling mildly obscene good-byes to his crew, Brad stuck the envelope in his journal and put them both in his jacket pocket.

"Safe travels, Coach," he yelled across the room.

The Leadership Moment

B rad pushed hard through the traffic on Highway 101 as he made his way toward the Imperial Hotel in downtown San Francisco for the NPC annual awards banquet. The big day had finally arrived. More than five hundred of the company's top executives were gathered in the ballroom of one of the swankiest hotels in the city—and it looked for all the world like the winner of the event's biggest award would arrive late.

"The Sales Leader of the Year ought to buy himself one of these stupid monkey suits," Brad said to himself, referring to the tuxedo he'd had to rent. He exited the highway and sat anxiously waiting for the light to change.

The tux rental is what had put him behind schedule. The formalwear store had sent the wrong suit over, and Brad quickly decided he'd rather arrive late than dress in teal and look like a 1970s lounge singer. By the time he took it back, got the right tux, changed, and drove to the hotel, he had already missed the salads, and the main course was being served.

The people on Brad's team—who'd been invited to attend so they could see him receive the award—were seated at a table near the back of the room. Brad noticed them from across the room as soon as he walked in. He gave them a quick nod and wave as he hurriedly made his way toward a table at the front. They obligingly returned the wave and went back to buttering their rolls.

Brad took his seat, apologizing to his tablemates for his tardiness. Suddenly it hit him: In his rush to resolve the tux fiasco, he'd forgotten to open the envelope Coach had given him before leaving for Europe. He pulled his journal from his jacket pocket, slid out the envelope, and opened it. Inside, he found a handwritten, heartfelt congratulatory note from Coach.

"Not hungry?" asked Jan Muller, the senior vice-president of operations for NPC.

The question startled Brad, who'd been lost in thought as he reflected on Coach's letter.

"Oh, no; I had a late lunch," Brad said, looking up from the note. "I'm not very hungry."

He downed the glass of iced tea in front of him, trying to bring life to his dry throat. He made a feeble attempt to join in the group's conversation to hide the fact that his stomach was doing flip-flops. As the awards ceremony began, Brad's palms were sweating, his heart was racing, and his mind was drifting back to the coaching conversations he'd had with Coach over the past few weeks. His mind was in a fog when he heard the applause and realized it had followed his name that was being announced by NPC's CEO, Martin Cower.

"And for the final award of the evening, it brings me great pleasure to introduce our Sales Leader of the Year . . . Brad Hutchinson!" Cower announced.

With his adrenaline pumping and his speech in hand, Brad slowly walked up to the podium. As the applause finally died down, Brad looked across the now-silent room filled with the "who's who" of his company's power players, all dressed to the nines. Suddenly it was as if the scene had switched into slow motion. He could hear his heart pounding, and his breathing speeded up. His sweaty palms tightly clutched the speech he had labored over.

As he arrived at the podium, Brad looked down at his speech notes. *I can't do this*, he thought as he glanced over the notes one last time. *This just isn't me anymore.* With a fresh wave of courage and inspiration, he took a deep breath and began. "A wise man once told me . . ."

Abruptly, Brad stopped. His voice had cracked. He

cleared his throat and started again, this time a little louder and directly into the microphone.

"A wise man once told me to get it out of my head and into my heart," he said. "So here goes—"

With that, he crinkled up the speech and tossed it over his shoulder, drawing light laughter from the crowd.

"When I first became a manager," he said, "I thought I had all the answers. Now I realize that's not my job. My job is to ask all the right questions. When I first became a manager, I thought my job was to make my number. I was wrong. I now realize that my job is to help my *team members* make *their* number. When I first became a manager, I thought it was all about me. I was wrong. I now realize it's about *them*—my team."

Brad pointed to the table at the back of the room where his team was sitting and called out each person by name.

"I now realize it's about helping my team achieve *their* dreams, *their* goals, and *their* aspirations. It's about helping them grow and improve so that *they* can achieve *their* potential—as professionals and as human beings."

Brad took another breath but his pause was brief.

"And while the scoreboard may indicate that I've succeed as a sales manager," he said, "the truth is, I now realize that I've failed as a sales leader. I've learned a lot over the past few weeks and I now realize that I've been wrong about a lot of things. But there's one thing I know I'm right about—and that's that I am not worthy of this award. You see, I'd gladly accept it if it weren't for one word. It doesn't say sales *manager*, it says sales *leader*. So as much as I sincerely appreciate the acknowledgment, I'm afraid I must respectfully decline the award."

A wave of shock rolled over the audience, beginning with the look on CEO Martin Cower's face and working its way to the back of the room where Brad's team sat in stunned silence. A murmur of whispers quickly filled the ballroom as the people at each table began wondering out loud: "Is this really happening?"

With Coach's letter still fresh in his mind, Brad added one final thought.

"A wise man once told me that when all is said and done and we've finally completed this journey we call life, what will matter most is not what we have achieved, but rather who we have become," Brad said with renewed confidence. "And while I realize I have a *long* way to go to reach my potential both as a person and as a leader"—he paused, overcome with emotion as he realized he'd seized the moment—"I think I'm finally at least reading from the right playbook."

With that, Brad turned from the podium, stepped off the stage, and walked through the center of the crowded ballroom toward the back doors. A few sporadic claps finally broke the awkward silence then quickly exploded into a roaring applause, and, by the time he had reached the exit, a standing ovation.

Stepping into the cool Bay Area evening, Brad thought to himself, *Great—now what?* After considering his options, he smiled and said, "What else?"

An hour or so later Brad walked into Halftime. The bar was filled with a typical Friday evening crowd. He parked himself at the bar, ordered a pint, and began chatting with Little Nikki and a few regulars he'd gotten to know over the past few weeks. The familiar surroundings helped him sense Coach's presence, but he couldn't help wondering what the old man was doing at that particular moment in Europe.

After finishing his first pint, Brad excused himself from the small talk and made his way to the restroom. He stood over the old tin horse trough, perusing last week's sports sections that were pinned to the corkboard in front of him. Without warning, the door behind him flew open and slammed against the wall.

"Now that's a *real* fancy suit you got on there!" bellowed a loud, familiar voice. "Don't you think you're a little overdressed for a sh-- hole like this? What, you just come from a funeral or somethin'?" Coach's raucous laughter echoed off the walls.

Brad just about fell over. "What are *you* doing here?" he shouted. "I thought you were still in Europe!"

"Just got back a couple of hours ago," Coach said. "We ended up getting the deal done sooner than expected, so I decided to cut the trip a little short. I probably would've made it in time for your big award if it hadn't been for a weather delay in Chicago."

Coach paused and looked at his newest protégé. "So how did it go, kid?"

Brad desperately wanted to unload all the details about how he had seized his leadership moment and had declined the award, because he knew how proud Coach would be of him. But for some reason, it just didn't feel right.

"Ah, it was uneventful," he said. "You know how boring those stupid things are."

With a twinkle in his eye and a knowing smile on his face, Coach put his hand on Brad's shoulder as they walked out of the restroom. He pointed back to the pool tables, where a large group of Coach's crew had gathered.

"Come on, why don't you come on over and join us?"

As he started toward the pool tables, Coach noticed

something out of the corner of his eye. A group of about ten young professionals all dressed to the hilt had just walked into the bar; they were standing in the entrance, scanning the place as if they were looking for someone in particular.

"On second thought, Sales Leader," Coach said as he patted Brad on the back and directed his attention toward the front door, "it looks like some friends came to help you celebrate after all."

The Story Behind the Story

WHENEVER I GIVE A keynote or workshop, I'm often asked about the inspiration behind Brad and Coach—and whether the story you just read is true. In celebration of this new edition of *The Weekly Coaching Conversation*, I want to share with you a bit of the story behind the story.

It all started just about the time my team and I were about two-thirds of the way through our research project on employee performance. While we had not yet drawn any definitive conclusions from the data, we had already made a number of surprising breakthroughs that I'll share with you in the next section.

I decided to share some of our preliminary findings with a few friends and colleagues in the industry. One of those people was Ken Blanchard—a friend and mentor of mine, someone for whom I have a tremendous amount of respect.

One morning I was sitting with Ken at his kitchen table and we were reviewing the research. He turned to me and said he thought we were onto something big—and that I should write a fable.

This seemed logical enough. That has obviously worked out pretty well for Ken. There was only one problem: I had absolutely no idea how to write a fable. Creativity just wasn't my strong suit. I'm more of a business-minded, analytical type. Truth be told, I don't even read fiction!

Despite my initial apprehension, I decided to at least give it a try. But after weeks of racking my brain for a storyline, nothing came. I was starting to get frustrated and was about to give up on the idea—until fate intervened.

As luck would have it, not too long thereafter I was scheduled to take my family on a weeklong Disney Cruise in the Caribbean. What better place to find a little creative inspiration than on a Disney Cruise, right?

I don't know if you've ever been on a cruise—especially a Disney Cruise—but they're not exactly conducive to getting work done. It seemed every time I managed to sneak away to a quiet spot on the ship for a little brainstorming, Mickey Mouse would pop around the corner or Tinkerbelle would flutter by followed by a swarm of screaming kids. Not exactly an idyllic writer's retreat.

Having made zero progress and already being halfway through the trip, I relented, decided to pack my journal away, and vowed to just enjoy the rest of the vacation with my family.

Later that evening—in the middle of the night—I woke from a deep sleep. My eyes popped wide open. *I've got it!* I jumped out of bed, grabbed my journal, and managed to scamper through the cabin and out onto the balcony without waking any of my family.

I'll never forget that night. Even as I write this, I can still see it. The moon was bigger and brighter than I had ever seen, and the crystal-clear, blue Caribbean water was literally glowing. It was magical.

I sat down, opened my journal, and started furiously writing: Act 1 . . . Act 2 . . . Act 3 . . . The story was coming together in my mind faster than I could capture it on paper—which was rare for me, as I honestly struggle with writing. But strangely enough, the story didn't come to me as a book; it came to me as a movie. In my mind's eye, I could see Brad and Coach sitting at the bar enjoying a couple of pints and developing this rather unique relationship. At the time, I was simply trying to capture snap shots of the coaching conversation between these two characters and then weave in bits and pieces of the framework where possible.

In hindsight, I now realize that the reason this story flowed through me so effortlessly is because, in many respects, the story you just read is really my story. It's me acting as Coach—knowing what I've learned, studied, and experienced—having a conversation with the me of twenty years ago, when I first started managing and learning about leadership.

Fortunately, I didn't get stood up by my team at a dive bar like Brad did. But there was one transformational event early in my management career that has had a profound impact on my life and was a big part of the inspiration behind writing this book.

I was in my mid-twenties and was managing close to a $100 million business for a publically traded company. I'd just been selected as the Worldwide Sales Manager of the Year, and I was about to be promoted to be a member of the management committee. But before I officially transitioned into my new role, I decided to have my team over for a little celebratory sendoff.

Life was good. I was newly married, had just bought a new house, and my career was taking off. So my wife and I decided to pull out all the stops for a party—fancy hors d'oeuvres, open bar, live music, the whole nine yards. The evening was a hit and everyone seemed to be having a blast.

Everyone, that is, except for me, because of what happened as the evening drew to a close.

Things had finally died down and there were only about a dozen or so of my team members left in the backyard.

We were telling jokes, sharing funny stories, laughing, and just having a great time.

Just about the time the music stopped, one of my team members turned to me—with everyone listening in—and, in a dead serious tone, said, "You know, Brian . . . You're actually a really cool guy . . . outside of the office."

Silence. I think even the crickets stopped chirping. You could have heard a pin drop as everyone on my team turned to me, nervously awaiting my response.

While I was obviously stunned by the comment, I didn't want to make a scene, so I decided to just laugh it off and play along with a little self-deprecating humor. Unfortunately, this only seemed to make matters worse. Perhaps partially inspired by a little liquid courage and the fact that I was no longer their boss, other team members started to chime in with some of their "funny" stories about me and my management approach. I just laughed and continued to play it off as if it didn't matter—but it did. It mattered a lot.

Later that evening, after everyone had left, I was upstairs washing my face and getting ready for bed. I remember staring into the mirror for a long time. Eventually my eyes started to well up when, for the first time, I didn't recognize—or like—the person staring back at me.

In psychology, this is called *self-deception*. In other

words, you have a problem, but the *real* problem is that you don't realize you have a problem. Well, I can assure you, I was under no illusion after that evening. I knew I had a problem—a big problem.

For the first time, I became aware that my maniacal focus on driving results and getting things done had unintended consequences. Sure, I was succeeding, but at what cost?

While acknowledgment of this problem was a giant step in the right direction, there was another big problem: I had absolutely no idea where to turn for a solution. I started devouring every management book I could get my hands on and attending every leadership workshop I could find, but nothing worked.

Not too long thereafter, I did what any world-class leader would do . . . I quit! My wife and I sold our house and we went on worldwide sabbatical, which ultimately culminated in me writing my first book, *Become Who You Were Born to Be*.

You see, as altruistic as this may sound, I've honestly always had a very strong sense of purpose—I've always believed that I was put on this earth to make a positive difference in peoples' lives. And I now realize that at the time I was just too naïve, and perhaps too stupid, to realize that being a manager—or better yet, a leader—provides the perfect platform to do just that.

Fast-forward to today. After more than a decade of researching successful people, leaders, teams, and organizations and after a career as a management consultant and the founder of a couple of startup companies, I now realize that "my story" has, ironically enough, come full circle.

If I had known then what I know now, there's a very good chance I would never have quit that job. Instead, I probably would have stayed on the corporate path—which would have been a heck of a lot easier than the path I've taken. But that obviously wasn't meant to be. I guess the Man had a different plan, and I needed to personally experience back then what I now teach today.

I hope by now you get the sense that this is a topic that I'm incredibly passionate about. Not only is this something that I've studied academically and experienced professionally, but, more important, I've lived it personally. My hope is that in some small way this book and my story will prove to be a catalyst in ensuring that your story has an even happier ending.

THE
PROGRAM

"In all cases, weekly coaching vastly improved employee productivity."

—Timothy Keningham, PhD
Global Chief Strategy Officer and EVP, IPSOS

Research Overview

As a management consultant during the aftermath of the global financial crisis of 2008, I was curious to see how organizational leaders were adapting to the proverbial "new normal." After speaking to dozens of *Fortune* 500 company leaders, it quickly became apparent that they were all focused on one thing: organic productivity.

In other words, they had shifted their focus from resource allocation to resource optimization, and they were looking for new and innovative ways to drive more growth and more improvement from within their existing organizations.

With that in mind, my team and I, along with Ipsos—one of the world's leading research firms—started on what turned out to be an exhaustive five-year research project. While we initially focused on sales, we quickly expanded our research to include all functional areas once we began to understand the magnitude and universal nature of the problem. Ultimately, our study encompassed more than two thousand managers and employees from companies ranging in size from Global 2000 to small and medium-sized businesses (SMBs).

Realizing that the first step to solving a problem is to define it correctly, my research team and I set out to find the answer to one seemingly simple question: Why aren't employees more productive?

As the following chart illustrates, we discovered that there are four main reasons:

Lack of Efficiency (or Focus)

Perhaps the single most pervasive problem plaguing employee productivity is a lack of efficiency or focus. The vast majority of employees come to work intending to get a lot done, but without a system to help minimize distractions and maximize focus, they end up squandering precious time *reacting* instead of *acting*. There's a lot of input (activity) but very little output (results). They're working hard but they're working on the wrong things—and as a result, they have very little to show for their efforts. This problem is compounded as organizational leaders continually pile on more and more for their employees to do with fewer and fewer resources.

There's an equally troubling side effect to lack of efficiency. Over time, as employees inevitably tire from working hard and having little to show for their efforts, they become discouraged, get burned out, and stop trying so hard—which is the second biggest issue we discovered.

• • •

Lack of Effort (or Work Motivation)

This could best be summed up by the anecdotal response we received from countless employees: "I give 100 percent to my boss . . . about 50 percent of the time." In fact, our research revealed that *one in four employees reported that they were consistently performing at less than 50 percent of potential.* I know what you're probably thinking: *How can you measure someone's potential? It's completely subjective.* And you're right.

But that's not the point. The point is that employees are telling us that they have more to give. So the fundamental question becomes what you—as a manger, supervisor, or team leader—have to do to get it out of them.

More to the point, we began to analyze *why* most employees weren't giving their best to their boss. This led us to begin studying what role a manager's level of engagement and feedback (or lack thereof) played in the amount of discretionary effort the team members put forth. After all, effort is the keystone to success. Or as Winston Churchill put it, "Continuous effort—not strength or intelligence—is the key to unlocking our potential."

Lack of Accountability (or Follow-through)

This is an interesting dynamic: Team members know what to do and how to do it—they just *don't* do it. While some in this group are actively disengaged, we discovered that many are actually well intentioned. In other words, they want to get things done, but continually lose focus and fail to follow through given the whirlwind of activities, tasks, and fire drills constantly being thrown at them on a daily basis.

Surprisingly, "lack of accountability" in most cases appeared to be less of a motivation problem and more of a "systems" problem. We discovered that most managers don't have a closed-loop system where they follow up with their team members on a regular cadence to make sure they're on track for achieving their goals and to hold them accountable. Most managers tell their team members what to do, assume they're doing it, and then follow up months later just before the deadline only to discover that their team members had drifted off course long ago.

• • •

Lack of Ability (or Effectiveness)

We were shocked to discover that both employees and managers ranked this category the lowest. After all, with so many billions of dollars spent each year on frontline employee skills training, we assumed that a lack of ability (or skill deficiency) would be one of the biggest performance inhibitors. In fact, a recent McKinsey study[2] found that frontline managers receive the least amount of training and development (9 percent) while frontline employees receive the most (27 percent).

Interestingly enough, if you parse through the research data, you'll discover that the fundamental problem paralyzing employee performance is not necessarily an employee *skillset* issue—it's an employee *behavioral* issue. A study[3] published by Bain & Company corroborated our findings and reported that "65% of initiatives required significant behavior change on the part of frontline employees, something that leaders fail to anticipate and plan for in advance."

---

[2] De Smet, A., McGurk, M., and Vinson, M. 2010. McKinsey survey results: How companies manage the front line today. New York: McKinsey & Company.

[3] Litre, P., Bird, A., Carey, G., & Meehan, P. January 12, 2011. Results delivery®: Busting three common myths of change management. Insights.

$$\frac{\text{Employee Productivity} =}{\text{Efficiency x Effort x Effectiveness}}$$

$$\text{Accountability}$$

This prompted us to start analyzing what role these world-class leaders of high-performance teams played in shaping the behaviors of their team members—which led us to yet another breakthrough: The *real* reason most employees aren't more productive actually has a lot less to do with the employees themselves and a lot more to do with their managers.

To put it differently, you could just as easily replace "accountability" in the above equation with "manager," because the manager is the common denominator and the key to simultaneously initiating and *sustaining* improvement in all three areas. Yet it's amazing that the same McKinsey study revealed that only 10 percent of companies believe their frontline managers are prepared to successfully coach, develop, and lead their teams.

As we began conducting a meta-analysis to compare our research findings with those of other studies, a picture began to slowly emerge. The deeper we looked into the data, the more we became convinced that we had stumbled onto something big.

On a hunch, we decided to shift the focus of our research.

We stopped asking, "Why aren't employees more productive?" and started asking, "Why are most managers only able to get so little out of their teams?"

And that's when it hit us: The fundamental difference between leaders of highly productive teams and most managers didn't necessarily come down to what most would suspect: their IQ, strategic vision, or operational prowess. The fundamental difference primarily came down to one thing: their approach. These elite leaders of high-performance teams and organizations didn't act like managers. They acted like coaches.

Like coaches, leaders of high-performance teams understand that the only way to *systematically* improve performance is through consistently giving constructive coaching and developmental feedback. In fact, dozens of studies—including our own—have proven that there's a direct correlation between the quantity and quality of coaching a person receives and his or her level of performance improvement.

In other words, a lot of coaching equals a lot of improvement. A little coaching equals a little improvement. And no coaching equals no improvement. This seems pretty obvious, right?

Well, listen to this: we discovered that *44 percent of employees report never receiving any constructive coaching or developmental feedback.* That's right—nearly half of

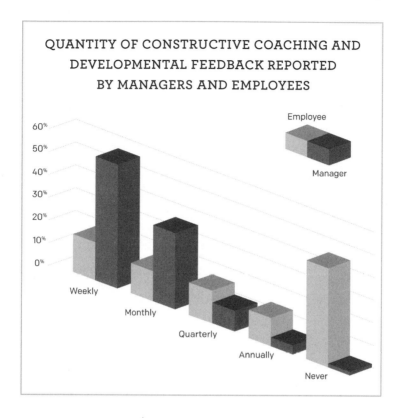

QUANTITY OF CONSTRUCTIVE COACHING AND
DEVELOPMENTAL FEEDBACK REPORTED
BY MANAGERS AND EMPLOYEES

all employees aren't receiving *any* constructive coaching or developmental feedback! That's a staggering figure, and it begs the next logical question.

Why *aren't* most employees receiving much, if any, coaching? Better yet, why aren't more managers coaching and developing their teams? It turns out the answer is actually pretty simple: When it comes to the people side of management, they've never been taught the right approach.

Management Approach
MATRIX

As Coach explained in the fable, we discovered that there are basically four different types of managers. And each type of manager has a very distinctive style or approach that impacts the rapport with team members and the team members' level of productivity.

The four types of managers include the Nice-Guy Manager, the Micromanager, the Do-It-All Manager, and the Coach. Unlike the other three types of managers, the Coach manages to maintain a high level of rapport with his or her team members while still consistently getting the most out of them—often twice as much as most managers.

We discovered that there are two key distinctions that separate these world-class leaders of high-performance teams—or coaches—from most managers: their mindset and their skillset.

For example, in the eyes of most managers, you have organizational goals on the one hand and people development goals on the other. Most managers view them as separate and distinct goals with separate and distinct strategies. In fact, most managers are so focused on organizational goals that they completely disregard people development goals, outsourcing those to HR.

Coaches, on the other hand, have a completely different philosophy. They don't view organizational goals and people development goals as separate and distinct—they view them as one and the same. They superimpose the two. In other words, they believe that the way to achieve organizational goals *is through people development*.

They understand that a manager's job isn't done once you find the right people and put them into the right seats. In fact, it's just beginning. They understand that developing their team isn't just HR's job—it's *their* job. In fact, it's perhaps their single most important job. They understand that giving constructive coaching and developmental feedback isn't just something that takes place during annual or quarterly performance reviews. It's an ongoing process that should be inextricably integrated into everything a manager does on a *weekly* basis.

If there's anything I've learned about research, it's that when you ask a better question, you typically get a better answer. So with this in mind, we became laser-focused on finding the answer to perhaps the most important question of all: What is the one thing managers must do in order to *systematically* improve their team's performance?

While there are countless things a manager could do to incrementally improve his or her team's performance, that wasn't our focus. With surgical precision, we were focused on pinpointing the high-leverage point where a manager could *systematically* improve their team's performance and drive massive improvement with the least amount of time, energy, effort, or change required.

Having devoted years to studying best practices and codifying those critical few key behaviors, tools, tactics, and strategies that will really help you move the needle on your team's performance, we've distilled it all into a simple-to-understand, easy-to-apply, three-step framework. The result is the foundation of the Weekly Coaching Conversation framework, which we'll briefly introduce in the next section.

Framework Overview

I recently sat down with David Covey—son of the late, great Stephen Covey and former COO of Franklin Covey—and took him through an in-depth review of the Weekly Coaching Conversation (WCC) training system. I have to admit, I was a bit nervous. After all, here was a guy who was not only extremely bright, but had literally been in and around the training business his entire life. If anyone had a pulse on the industry and a unique vantage point from which to judge how our training program stacked up against all the rest, it was definitely David.

After I took him through a thorough review of the program, David sat back with a contemplative look on his face and paused, while I anxiously sat there awaiting the verdict. To my surprise (and relief), he said that he would give our WCC program an A+ relative to all the other training programs he's seen.

While I was obviously flattered by the compliment, I was curious as to why he was so enthusiastic. So I asked him. He responded with something I'll never forget. He said, "My father [Stephen Covey] always used to say: If you want to create incremental change, focus on the behavior; if you want to create quantum change, focus on the paradigm."

David went on to say that the WCC program was not only "world-class," but more importantly, it was "paradigm shifting." And while I hadn't managed to articulate it with quite as much panache as Stephen Covey did, as soon as David quoted his father I realized that subconsciously this had actually been my goal all along.

Through my research over the years, I've learned that if we could fundamentally shift a person's paradigm—or, in our case, the way in which people perceive themselves, their role, and their team—the desired behavioral change would start to happen automatically. I knew that if we really wanted the behavioral change to stick, we had to first address the *mindset* (how they think) before we address the *skillset* (what they do).

This is why the first step of the framework, "Change your Approach," is so important—and, frankly, it's a main reason why so many manager-as-a-coach programs fail. Most programs attempt to address the skillset without first addressing the mindset. In other words, most

Weekly Coaching Conversation®
MANAGER MODULE

programs fail to address the underlying beliefs that are controlling the behavior and fail to take a *systematic* approach to solving the problem.

For example, as long as you continue to "see" yourself as a manager, you will continue to act like a typical manager. But through using various strategies of influence, when we are able to fundamentally shift your paradigm and get you to see yourself in a totally different way—as a "coach"—you will inevitably start to act like a coach. And the more you continue see yourself as a coach and act like a coach, something miraculous starts to happen: You *become* one.

Step 1: Change your Approach

How would you classify your current management approach? Be honest. Would you say that you're more of a Nice-Guy Manger . . . a Do-It-All Manager . . . a Micromanager . . . a Coach?

Whenever I ask this question during my keynotes or workshops, I usually get the same response: "Well, it depends on the situation. You can't really put me in a box." That's funny, because when I ask their *team members* the same question, they seem to have no problem putting their boss in a box—and it's rarely in the upper right-hand quadrant.

The truth is, while your behavior may vary slightly depending on the situation, you do have a distinctive management approach, whether you realize it or not. And perhaps more than anything else, your management approach is having the most profound impact on your team's performance—and, by default, your career.

I don't know about you, but this was a revelation to me. To be honest, I used to think that there were only two types of managers: producers and non-producers. To me, defining success as a manager was simple: either you delivered results or you did not deliver results. I didn't used to care *how* the results were achieved or even *who* achieved them, as long as we got the job done. *Do whatever it takes to make it happen* used to be my management philosophy.

Sound familiar? Well, based on our research findings, it should—because it pretty much sums up how the vast majority of managers think today. When you ask thousands of managers what their job is and you analyze the data as we've done, you'll see that most managers respond with an answer along these lines: *My job is to deliver results.* Or, in Brad's case, "My job is to make my number."

This paradigm shift in thought process that we need to create could perhaps best be summarized by Coach's response when he said to Brad, "Your job is not to make *your* number; it's to help your team members make *theirs*."

While the play on words is subtle, the distinction between these two opposing viewpoints and the corresponding impact your behavior has on your team's performance is profound. You can make significant strides toward becoming a coach by shifting your perspective and changing the answer to one simple question: *What is my job?*

OLD DEFINITION: My job as a manager is to deliver results.

NEW DEFINITION: My job as a coach is to consistently get the most out of my team and to *systematically* improve their performance.

Let me be clear: I'm not saying that your job is *not* to deliver results, because that obviously *is* your job. What I'm saying is that the best way to consistently deliver results *is through consistently coaching and developing you people.* And I'm not referring to once-a-year check-the-box training either. I'm talking about you making the intellectual and emotional leap to realize that your new job—as a coach—is to *systematically* improve your team's performance by constantly observing, evaluating, challenging, questioning and coaching your team members to give their very best each and every day.

Tactical Takeaway:

Spend the next week or so analyzing your current management approach and acting as an objective observer of your daily habits and routines. How much of your day do you spend on the people side versus the process side of

MOST MANAGERS . . .

- Focus only 30 percent on the people side of management and 70 percent on the process side
- Believe that talent is primarily something you acquire
- Believe you either "have it" or you don't
- Focus too much on the results and too little on improving the process that produces the results
- Struggle to find the right balance and are either too engaged (Micromanager) or too disengaged (Nice Guy Manager and/or Do-It-All Manager)
- Don't understand the connection between their management approach and their team's performance

WORLD-CLASS COACHES . . .

- Focus 70 percent on the people side of management and 30 percent on the process side
- Believe that talent can be developed
- Believe that each and every team member is capable of performing at a higher level and that it's their job to help their team members realize their potential
- Are manically focused on improving the process that produces the results
- Find the right level of engagement with each team member to consistently get the most out of them
- Understand the connection between their management approach and their team's performance

management? How engaged are you with your team members, and what's the quality of the conversations you're having with your team members—from *their* perspective? Write down your insights in your journal.

Second, as far as your mindset is concerned, there are two key beliefs you *must* change in order to become a coach. In short, you must believe that your team has more to give, and that it's your job to get it out of them.

And finally, one of the most important things you need to do in order to change your approach is to become approachable—which leads us to the second step of the framework.

Step 2: Create the Environment

Have you ever had someone try to give you some "friendly advice" but you didn't hear it because you didn't really trust the person or his or her motives? Well, we discovered that the same holds true with the dynamics between managers and their team members in the workplace.

Our research revealed something that, while deceptively simple, is often overlooked: Before you can facilitate a constructive coaching conversation, you must first create an environment that's conducive to coaching.

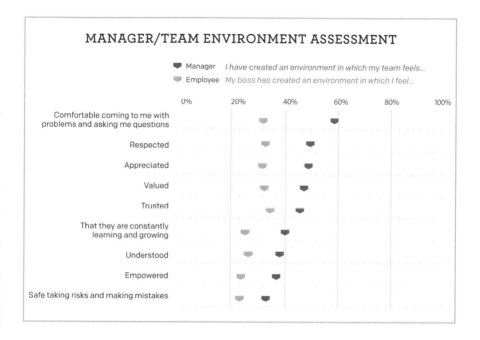

After all, coaching skills are useless if your team members aren't coachable (which, incidentally, is why the WCC Team Member module is so invaluable to helping team members buy into the WCC system.)

We were shocked to discover that—by their own admission—most managers have quite a bit of work to do in this area. In short, if your team members aren't feeling respected, appreciated, valued, trusted, understood, empowered, or safe, it's obvious that they won't be very receptive to having a coaching conversation. But keep in mind that this is only the first step. To get to the next level and become a

MOST MANAGERS . . .

- Haven't created an environment that's conducive to coaching
- Care more about results than their people
- Have unintentionally created a "go-to environment" in which team members:
  - Do not feel safe coming to them with questions, concerns, or admitting mistakes
  - Do not share honest opinions with them for fear of reprisal
  - Do not proactively come to them for fear of looking weak, incompetent, or ill prepared

WORLD-CLASS COACHES . . .

- Work hard to create—and maintain—an environment that is conducive to coaching
- Care about their people, have their best interests in mind, and genuinely want them to succeed
- Have intentionally created a "come-to environment" in which team members:
  - Feel safe coming to them with questions or concerns and/or feel safe admitting mistakes
  - Openly share opinions with them—even negative ones
  - Proactively come to them asking for coaching

world-class coach, you've got to get your team members to not only be "open" to having a coaching conversation, but to proactively come to you *asking* for it, because they realize it's the only way they're going to take their game to the next level.

Tactical Takeaway:

It is critical that you immediately start taking steps toward creating a safe environment in which your team members can try, come up short, receive coaching, and try again. Given that the first step toward change is awareness, we've designed a simple questionnaire to help you assess the level of rapport you have with your team and to determine whether you've done a good job of creating the type of environment that is conducive to coaching.

Rate yourself on each of the following questions using a score of 1 to 5, with 5 being the highest and 1 being the lowest.

_____ Do my team members trust me and believe that I genuinely have their best interests in mind?

_____ Do my team members feel safe coming to me with questions and admitting mistakes?

_____ Do my team members feel valued by me?

_____ Do my team members feel that I appreciate their hard work and effort?

_____ Do my team members feel understood by me?

_____ Do my team members feel respected by me?

_____ Do my team members feel empowered by me?

Add up your total and write the number in the blank space provided.

Use the key to diagnose the level of rapport you think you have with your team members. For maximum impact, have your team members complete the diagnostic as well to better understand their assessment of the type of environment you've created. Compare and contrast the results and use the findings as a basis for a "pull-the-weeds" conversation as referenced in the fable.

33–35 EXCELLENT—Keep up the great work!

28–32 VERY GOOD—One or more areas could use improvement.

21–27   GOOD—Several areas could use
         improvement.

14–20   FAIR—All areas could use improvement.

7–13   POOR—You may want to find a new
         position. :)

Step 3: Transform the Conversation

From time to time, I get a bit of pushback from a skeptical manager who essentially says, "I don't need to have a *weekly* coaching conversation with my team members. I talk to them all the time."

I typically respond by asking, "And what's the value of those conversations—from your team members' perspective?

I'm usually met with a long, uncomfortable silence followed by a dazed and confused look on their face.

I then explain that having observed hundreds of these typical manager/team member conversations over the years, I actually agree that most managers *do* talk to their team members with some regularity. But having done the research, I also understand how most team members perceive the value of these interactions. In general, these conversations are perceived at one extreme as being congenial but meaningless (Nice-Guy Manager), and at the other extreme directive, demanding, degrading, and/or downright contentious (Micromanager and/or Do-It-All Manager).

But then we stumbled onto this rare breed of world-class leader who had a completely different approach. These leaders managed to stay engaged, but not too engaged. They were nice, but they weren't too nice. And they too had regular interaction with their team members—but these conversations weren't unstructured and all over the map like most that we observed. These coaching conversations were more focused. There was a certain flow, a rhythm, a definitive process and set cadence to them.

They weren't warm and fuzzy career-development conversations, nor did they feel like the dreaded performance review conversations. They were short, to the point, and productive. The vibe was typically comfortable and positive but at times it could get pretty intense.

And perhaps more important, the data revealed that the recipients of these "weekly coaching conversations" were more engaged, motivated, efficient, effective—and *a lot* more productive. In fact, our research revealed that on average these coaches got twice as much out of their team members than do most managers.

MOST MANAGERS . . .

- Focus on judgment and blame through negative reinforcement
- Talk 80 percent of the time and listen only 20 percent of the time
- Do not hold team members accountable to a high performance standard
- Rarely get the most out of their team

WORLD-CLASS COACHES . . .

- Focus on improvement and growth through positive reinforcement
- Talk only 20 percent of the time and listen 80 percent of the time
- Hold team members accountable to a high performance standard
- May not always have the best people, but almost always get the best out of the people they have

What was their secret? Well, having spent years searching for the answer and trying to codify the behaviors of these world-class coaches, we've distilled them into what we call the five critical coaching questions that you must help your team members answer in order to systematically improve their level of performance.

Five Critical Coaching Questions:

1. WHAT MUST THEY DO?

2. HOW SHOULD THEY DO IT?

3. DID THEY DO IT?

4. WHAT DID THEY DO RIGHT?

5. HOW CAN THEY IMPROVE NEXT TIME?

Why are these five critical coaching questions so *critical*? Because they directly map back to addressing the four biggest inhibitors to employee performance: a lack of efficiency (or focus), a lack of effort (or work motivation), a lack of effectiveness (or skill competency), and a lack of accountability (or follow-through). In other words, the specific skills and tools that we've modeled from these world-class coaches were uniquely designed to *simultaneously* drive improvement in all four areas—which is why it forms the foundation of the third step of the WCC framework.

Tactical Takeaways

This was a tough one. Frankly, there is so much more I want to teach you, I could easily write another book!

Instead of just giving you a few tactical takeaways and sending you on your way, I thought it might be more helpful if I actually taught you the specifics about how to begin the transformational process of becoming a world-class coach and how to facilitate a constructive coaching conversation. In fact, if you want to go deeper I've created an exclusive video training series that goes into great detail on these and many other important topics you won't want to miss. For a limited time, I'm allowing my readers to access this video training series—at no cost.

For instant access to this exclusive FREE video training series, go to
ProductivityDrivers.com/WCCInsiders/

• • •

Summary

Well, congratulations—you made it! I don't know about you, but I'm exhausted. Sitting down to synthesize and simplify more than five years of research and a lifetime of experience is no simple task. I sincerely hope that this isn't the end, but rather the beginning of our journey together as we help you take the next step toward becoming a world-class coach.

ACKNOWLEDGMENTS

This book has been many, many years in the making and would not have been possible without the incredible group of family, friends, and colleagues I have been so blessed to call my team.

First and foremost, my heartfelt thanks and gratitude to

- *my amazing wife, Claudia, for being my best friend since the day we met and for all her patience and support over the years. You are truly one in a million.*

- *my two beautiful girls, Grace and Giselle, for bringing so much joy and love into our lives.*

- *my parents, Larry and Sandy, for blessing me with the most amazing childhood one could hope for and for being the best "Bama" and "PePa" in the world. You are amazing.*

- *my siblings—Kevin, Jeff, and Ashley—for always being there. I'm so grateful our relationship has evolved and that we've been able to become such great friends over the years.*

- *my in-laws, George and Gudrun, for all the love and support you've given us over the years. We would not be where we are without you.*

I would also like to sincerely thank my world-class team, including

- *Martha Lawrence and Stephen Caldwell for your writing prowess.*
- *Bill Chiaravalle and his artistic touch on the cover design.*
- *Elyse Strongin and team at Neuwirth and Associates, Inc. for their masterful work on the interior design.*
- *Kathy Gordon and Angela Eschler for your attention to detail.*
- *Karen Kreiger and her team at Evolve for her early work and dedication to this book.*
- *my research team, especially Tim Keiningham and Luke Williams for their expertise and commitment to this research project.*
- *my entire ProductivityDrivers team for their tireless work and commitment to building world-class training products and programs that will continue to transform careers and change lives.*
- *all my coaches over the years—especially Ken Blanchard and Stephen Covey—for passing along your wisdom and example.*

- *and finally, Father Nick Dempsey for feeding my soul every Sunday at St. Therese and for inspiring me to use my God-given gifts to make a positive difference in people's lives.*

Without each and every one of you and all your help and support, I would not be able to achieve my dream of sharing this important message with the world. And so for this, I owe you a deep debt of gratitude.

ABOUT THE AUTHOR

BRIAN SOUZA is the president and founder of ProductivityDrivers, an innovative corporate training company specializing in improving employee performance and organizational productivity. As a respected thought leader in leadership development, employee performance, and sales, Souza is highly sought after as a keynote speaker and management consultant by top companies and organizations worldwide. Souza and his work have been featured in dozens of magazines and newspapers around the world, including *The European Business Review*, *Fast Company*, and *Success Magazine*. His first critically acclaimed book, *Become Who You Were Born to Be* (Random House, 2007), has been published in multiple languages around the world.

Brian lives in San Diego with his wife, Claudia, their two daughters, Grace and Giselle, and their dog, Gunnar.

To learn more, please visit ProductivityDrivers.com

Weekly Coaching Conversation®
Performance Improvement System

Rings of
Reinforcement

Structural Reinforcement

Management Reinforcement

Behavioral Reinforcement

WCC GOAL
Systematically
Improve Employee
Performance

WCC Team Member Training

WCC Manager Training

WCC Reinforcement Consulting

Productivity DRIVERS®
Training that Works

PRODUCTIVITYDRIVERS.COM

APPLYING THE WEEKLY COACHING CONVERSATION SYSTEM WITH YOUR TEAM OR ORGANIZATION

Weekly Coaching Conversation Manager Training Program

Are you ready to take that next critical step on *your* journey towards buildng a high-performance team and becoming a world-class coach? Register now for instant access to an exclusive FREE video training series that will go deep into the tactics, strategies, and frameworks discussed in this book.

Register now at ProductivityDrivers.com/WCCInsiders/

ADDITIONAL WCC SOLUTIONS:
- WCC Virtual Training Pilot
- WCC Team Member Training
- WCC Coach-to-Coach Reinforcement
- WCC Audio Program

ENGAGEMENT OPTIONS:
- Virtual Online Training
- Keynotes/Workshops
- In-houseTraining
- Train-the-Trainer (T3)

 Productivity**DRIVERS**™